7 THINGS CHRISTIANS NEED TO KNOW ABOUT ADDICTIONS

STEVE HORNE

HERITAGE BUILDERS PUBLISHING
MONTEREY, CLOVIS CALIFORNIA

HERITAGE BUILDERS PUBLISHING
© 2015

First Edition 2015

Contributing Editor, Lydia Howard
Cover Design by Rae House, Creative Marketing
Book Design, Nord Compo
Published by Heritage Builders Publishing
Clovis, Monterey California no zip code
www.HeritageBuilders.com   1-888-898-9563

ISBN 978-1-942603-29-0

Printed and bound in United States of America

HERITAGE BUILDERS

STATEMENT

....

This book is written in memory of those
who have lost their lives to addiction,
and to their families, starting with my own.

DEDICATION

....

To my son Sean, whose tragic death broke me into God's hands, and gave me a deep sense of compassion for people who lose children.

To my Savior & Lord, Jesus Christ, who suffered with me and used grief to break down the walls that were preventing the writing of this book.

To Dr. Sherman Smith and Heritage Builders Publishing, for opening the doors to a first time author and making it possible to see a vision become reality.

To Dale O'quinn, no finer a friend could anyone hope for, who has allowed me to invest my life in his.

To Bill Shade, who asked the right question, at the right time, in the right place, which gave the right motive, to write.

To the Addict that none of us have met, yet.

ACKNOWLEDGEMENTS

Nothing of lasting value can ever be accomplished without sacrifice. I thank my wife Sharon for her love, and supporting the commitment it took to write this book.

To our family, covering every shade of skin under the sun, blended together as one, separated only by death. We've never used the "step" word, it doesn't fit for us. Our walk through the valley of the shadow of death drew us closer, where in just a few short months my Mom died of cancer and our son Sean ended his own life. We are a family, and I thank all of you for determining that tragedy would only make us stronger.

To my Mom, who for several years attended a Recovery Sunday School Class that I taught, and one day said "I like the class, its strange learning from my Son. But if you hadn't of grown up in such a dysfunctional family you wouldn't know half of what you know". She was right. Mom was outspoken and told it like it was. Never had to wonder where I got it from. I didn't learn what I know in a classroom, life has taught me the hard lessons starting at a very early age.

Thanks Mom, for instilling in me the desire to achieve and never quit.

And Dad, for always providing for our family and teaching me the reality of a strong work ethic.

I never liked the process of learning what I know, but it made me who I am. The good, the bad, and the dysfunctional, God has used it all in my life. And for that, I am truly grateful.

11th Tradition

In honor of the 11th Tradition, this book does not speak for or represent any 12 Step Program.

CONTENTS

FOREWORD

....

By Dave Waters

This book is not for you...unless you know someone with an addiction or you are struggling with an addiction yourself.

I met my first recovering alcoholic as a five year old, son of a Pastor. That man (we'll call him Esteban to protect his identity) was found by my father as he lay intoxicated and playing a violin without strings on a street corner in Montevideo, Uruguay. While my father didn't know about the term recovery (as we call it today) he did know about grace, truth, love and compassion when he offered to buy the man some strings for his violin (which we later discovered he played wonderfully) and offered him a room and food in exchange for work. Slowly, Esteban became sober. I will never forget the process involved in bringing about his sobriety. Because I became a firm believer in transformation at a young age, I'm overjoyed at the privilege of introducing my friend Steve's excellent work on this very stubborn issue of addiction. I've found addiction present in every culture that I've ever observed.

Chances are that you do, in fact, know someone who is struggling with addiction. I've watched the suffering of those who live alongside the addicted as well, so you may have picked this book up thinking about a family member, a friend, a neighbor or a co-worker. Whatever the case, good for you!

Do you know what you need to know about addiction? I've not read a better book on addiction so I'd like to suggest that you're holding a wealth of accurate, thoughtful and well researched information.

Steve has, in my estimation, succeeded in setting a whole new direction for having a conversation in our culture about addiction. Chances are that some of what you will discover on these pages will collide with some of your own long held notions about addiction. Get ready for a healthy balance of grace and truth.

You won't be disappointed in Steve's approach. Throughout this book it is never his goal to heap on condemnation, but to point you toward the truth about addiction, thus allowing you to be convinced that there is great hope for you and/or someone you love who is addicted. While truth shines the light on our need, it is grace that applies truth so that transformation is possible. Steve's insights will help cast light on the shadowy world of addiction.

Without freeing anyone from the responsibility of taking the necessary steps to achieve recovery, this book will provide some solid direction on the journey to helping yourself or those you love.

Steve's manuscript is born from years of selflessly serving others with addiction. As I read through the book I recalled walking with him through some of his colorful illustrations. He was always careful to be both cunning and gentle as he attempted to help the addict, their loved ones, and even those observing from the sidelines. Those story moments happened as we served together in a great church in California. Steve served as the Pastor of the Recovery Ministry in the church where I was blessed to serve as the Senior Pastor. I've watched him help many people with their greatest need. The pages you are about to read are rich with that experience. When Steve contacted me about writing this foreword, I knew what the book would be about before he told me its title. Fourteen years ago, Steve told me that one day he would write a book about addiction. My words to him were

"Right on. Go for it"! He went on to explain to me that he knew that he didn't yet have what he needed to write that book about addiction, but would be writing it when the time was right. That time has arrived! Through these pages, you are the recipient of Steve's desire to serve the addicted and those who love them through a much larger venue. I'll leave you with this great book and one final thought…bad information is just as dangerous as no information at all. Given that fact, I'd encourage you to not settle for legalistic tradition, hearsay, rumor or anything else you might have read on the internet, but to dive right in to 7 Things Christians Need to Know about Addiction. You'll never look at an addict the same way again, even if it is yourself.

Dave Waters
Senior Pastor, Life Community Church
President, International Gospel Initiative
Alexandria, Virginia

PREFACE

....

September 5th, 2010, Sunday morning at Grace Chapel Church in Sanford, NC. About once a year I would be asked to "Preach" at the main service on Sunday mornings. That usually meant the Senior Pastor, Associate Pastor, Youth Pastor, and a few others were all going to be out at the same time. Kind of like being the 4th string quarter back, but that's OK because it's God's plan for me, I'm more of a Teacher that can Preach on occasion.

In praying and preparing for the service I asked God if I could put together a message, one that would encompass 25 years of experience in Recovery and Church. How could I summarize what I had learned over many years into a simple message that would help people? What should stay, what should go? There was a lot to think about, and I actually believe God gave me the idea in the first place then let me think that it was mine. What mattered most was that it was His will for that day.

The message given was "5 Things Christians Need to Know About Addiction", which included Chapters one - four and seven from this book. Chapters five & six were added during the writing of the manuscript, and came from years of research that had to be left out of the original message. The response on Sept. 5th was incredible. The altar was filled from side to side, prayers, tears, and God doing what He does, touching the hearts of people. There was more after the service as people came and responded with thanks. The Church service played on local television, one friend who never had an addiction said a week later that point #5 got him (seven in the book).

As part of my ministry work I spent several years on the Board of Directors of Overcomers Outreach International, eventually becoming the Chairman of the Board. As part of that experience I met Steve Arterburn who was the Chairman at the time I joined. He led a one day planning retreat and shared insights, direction, and experience. But of all the things he said that day one stuck with me more than others. He spoke about writing and developing resources to help people, and said "You never have to wonder which of your writings impacts people, you'll know by their response". Along with using some developed resources by others, I've been writing and teaching my own materials since 1998. Few have had the kind of impact as the original message. I have given that message several more times at various locations, but the response is always the same. It touches hearts.

"7 Things Christians Need to Know About Addiction" is a continuation of a seed God planted several years ago. It is my prayer that it continues to grow and produce results in the lives of people.

INTRODUCTION

....

The subject of addictions brings with it many opinions and concerns, as well as the harsh impact on the lives of those who struggle with it. The consequences can be fatal, as a person gradually destroys everything worthwhile in life including themselves. Christians who believe in the Bible as God's Holy Word, the infallible truth by which we live, also struggle to know if addictions are supported by the Scriptures. The pursuit of truth, or the denial of it, has led to varying opinions about what addiction is and how it can be remedied. Is it just a sin problem? Is it a matter of will power? If we can't find the word addiction in the Bible, is it really there? What is the truth?

So many questions, so many opinions. How does a person who has never had an addiction help their loved one break free? Many who seek help may not receive the best advice from people who don't really understand addiction but since they have the Bible they feel more than qualified to speak. The reasoning goes something like: *"I have a Bible, and the Bible has all truth, so everything I say is truth."* But that's not good enough. *A solution is only as good as it holds up under the worst of circumstances.*

Christian answers to addiction often do not hold up under the best of circumstances, and fail miserably under the worst. If it's just a matter of will power, then who needs Jesus? The truth is that it is not about will power. It is about God's power. Yet many

Christians today still use these same old statements that have been repeated over and over.

Then there's the examples of instant deliverance from addiction, ones that are pointed to as the only way God solves the problem. People who are delivered this way are held up in front of the church as proof of the singular method, and the ones who struggle to be delivered suffer while trying to find the same experience. Jesus once spoke words to a man who had just been healed instantly, and it wasn't the only time he spoke the same words. In Matthew Chapter Eight, He gave these instructions after performing a miracle: "*Jesus reached out his hand and touched the man. I am willing, he said. Be clean. Immediately he was cleansed of his leprosy. Then Jesus said to him: See that you don't tell anyone. But go, show yourself to the priest and offer the gift Moses commanded, as a testimony to them.*" Matthew 8:3-4.

This is the type of humble acceptance that people need today. If God decides to deliver someone from addiction instantly then what does that person have to be proud of? Praise, honor, and obedience to God would be good responses, but becoming an instant expert on how everyone else needs to be delivered? Certainly not. But is it really the instantly delivered who push this agenda? No, it's the Christians who are putting them on a pedestal, leaders in the church who probably think they're doing the right thing and honoring God. But are they?

I have met the fallen, the ones who were instantly delivered and relapsed with alcohol and drugs. When they fall, they fall hard, and usually don't get back up. I have met them inside and outside the U.S., they seem to be everywhere. The biggest problem with pushing instant deliverance as the only solution is there is no answer for relapse. The shame and guilt that a person feels is more than they can face, especially if they've been paraded around before the church. The problem is not instant deliverance as a method, it is that other methods are ignored, ones that God himself has provided. What Christians need to know about addiction goes way beyond instant deliverance.

The main Biblical support for understanding addiction is in Romans Chapter One. The apostle Paul was passionate about Rome, which means he knew of the sin that was present in its society. The culture was saturated with booze and drugs that equal or exceed what is available today. In the second half of Chapter One he writes about the extent of this sin and eventually points to the origin. *"They exchanged the truth about God for a lie, and worshiped and served created things rather than the Creator—who is forever praised. Amen."* Romans 1:25. *Worshipping the creation, rather than the Creator.*

It actually all started in the Garden of Eden God created and it didn't take man long to mess it up. Satan invited himself in and offered unlimited knowledge with the fruit of the tree. He brought doubt against God and introduced the first false belief that God didn't really mean what He said. Adam and Eve saw an opportunity to gain something, but it actually decreased life. God told them not to experience it, but they exchanged the truth for a lie. A problem entered from the outside, a seed of sin, which conceived and produced death. Satan has been using the same trick ever since, he just switches the substance from one to another. It starts with a thought, which leads to an action, and ends with consequences. *"What has been will be again, what has been done will be done again; there is nothing new under the sun."* Ecclesiastes 1:9.

All alcohol and drugs used by man to get high come from creation. Plants, vegetables, weeds, poppies, you name it and man has tried to get stoned from it. People drink, smoke, shoot, and snort, but it all has one thing in common, it enters a person from the outside and causes problems on the inside. Even non substance problems are stimulated from the outside; such as lust, gambling, and sex. The lustful desires are triggered from something the eye can see, or the senses can engage. The amount of creativity that mankind has put into satisfying the lust of his flesh is astonishing. Addiction is an accurate term.

The whole creation groans because of its condition of pain (Romans 8:22), therefore creation cannot bring healing; it can only provide more pain. People turn to creation to heal from the effects of sin. The result is temporary satisfaction, more sin, and more pain. Enough is never enough. Only the Creator can provide what is needed to heal the common problem of all mankind, a wounded soul. Everything else from creation produces dependency, chemical or otherwise.

"Do not love the world or anything in the world. If anyone loves the world, love for the Father is not in them. For everything in the world—the lust of the flesh, the lust of the eyes, and the pride of life—comes not from the Father but from the world. The world and its desires pass away, but whoever does the will of God lives forever." 1 John 2:15-17.

People today want to save everything but their own souls. Jesus provides the healing for a wounded spirit because He is eternal, not created. He took on a human form and healed the only part of creation that God wants to save, the souls of human beings. (Colossians 1:15-20, Luke 4:18-19, Romans 8:38, 39).

Addiction is not about will power or moral codes. It is about Satan destroying God's most precious creation. As Christians, we can't afford to simply be right in our own eyes. We have to do better. We have to do more.

God has provided a model of recovery that is rooted in Scripture and rejected by many Christians. It's a method of delivering people through a process, generically called "12 Step." At times this approach is credited to the devil, which is pure insanity. Jesus addressed this issue when they said the same about Him: *"Every kingdom divided against itself will be ruined, and every city or household divided against itself will not stand. If Satan drives out Satan, he is divided against himself. How then can his kingdom stand?"* Matthew 12:25-26.

Recovery attributes the works of faith to the power of God. It's a process that takes the works of Satan and transforms them, by using principles that originated in Scripture. Only the Bible can work for any culture, at any time, in any language, for any struggle people may have, and provide a spiritual solution to a problem in the flesh. Anything firmly rooted in the Bible will have the same potential. The success of recovery is the main proof of why it's not only *of* God, but it is *for* Christians. It's a process of purification that cleanses the soul.

On the other hand, there are people in recovery programs that need to know who Jesus Christ is and why He came to earth, died on the cross, and was resurrected from the grave. Eternity depends on it. And just as recovery programs have the answer to addiction for the church, Christians have the answer to eternal life for those in recovery.

This book is intended for a variety of audiences:
- People who do not understand addiction or its history, yet.
- The Christian sitting in the pew dying from addiction in silence.
- The recovering addict whose been told by Christians that their God is some nebulous being, but who knows that He is really a God of all power and knowledge.
- Addicts in faith based programs, 12-Step Recovery, or a combination of both.
- For the person in recovery who wants to know what else is required for eternity.
- The person who loves like Jesus loves, who hurts when people hurt, who wants to make a difference but does not know how.
- For the family of someone struggling with an addiction, who sees the failings of their current approach but doesn't know what else to do.

- This book is not for the few, the proud, the modern day Pharisees. Jesus couldn't get through to them back then and most likely He can't today. But there was one who came seeking truth. This book is for the Nicodemus', the ones who don't have all the answers, the ones seeking truth even when it doesn't make sense. It's for those who will come while it's still dark so they can find the light.
- It is for those who would change their opinion if it was their own son or daughter who becomes addicted, or dies from addiction. Would it have to go that far before a person accepts change?

In the chapters ahead, there are numerous testimonies of people who have struggled with addictions, Christians and non-Christians alike. The stories are true but the names have been changed to protect their identities, and will be referenced as such (i.e. John E. #1 and Jane E. #1). Their experiences are invaluable.

The Gospel is a simple solution to a complicated problem. Acceptance of the solution is our problem. Same as recovery, and the only thing that would keep people from learning is contempt.

"There is a principle which is a bar against all information, which is proof against all arguments and which cannot fail to keep a man in everlasting ignorance – that principle is contempt prior to investigation." Herbert Spencer.

One of the most visited subjects in the Bible that is surrounded by contempt before investigation is the wine Jesus made at the wedding in Canaan. It is surprising that there is even a question given the vast amount of simple proof that it was actually wine that contained alcohol. Christians who lack wisdom or the desire to investigate hold strongly to the position that is was grape juice. But this doesn't hold up under the truth.

First, the word "wine" used in John Chapter 2 is "oinos," a Greek word referring to a drink that has been fermented. Study any source of information on the process of fermentation and you will quickly learn that it produces ethanol, which is the alcohol content in wine. Preachers have been heard saying, "What Jesus made wasn't wine, it was fermented grape juice." This is a good example of contempt prior to investigation. The real miracle is that it was the best wine. Anybody could have stomped some grapes and produced juice that day, but Jesus made the quality of wine that takes several years to produce. Only He could have done that in one day, a true miracle. Take away this truth and you take away the miracle.

So it is with the subject of addiction. Beliefs are held onto in the church because they've been passed down through the generations. "What used to be called drunkenness is now called a disease." Contempt prior to investigation. The purpose of this book is to investigate the subject of addiction, and show good reason why there is something that Christians need to know.

CHAPTER ONE

Some People are Delivered in a Moment, Others are Delivered through a Process

II Kings Chapter 5 is a story of deliverance from the Old Testament of the Bible. It includes several people, but is primarily centered around Naaman, a great man, valiant warrior, captain to the king, and a leper. He was sick and searching for a solution, much like people today who hold great titles, run businesses, are fine Christians, and are addicts. Rarely are these people happy about their circumstances. They are sick and searching for a solution.

Naaman's story provides powerful insights which God intended for all generations. It begins with words coming from a nameless Israelite woman who provides the proper direction. The fact that she is so influential will continue to unfold as the story goes on. For now, she gives Naaman a referral to the God of Israel, the one true God. So Naaman goes to his king first, the King of Syria, and gets permission to leave. He is sent off with a personal letter from his king, a fine reference to validate how great he was. Along with the letter he takes ten talents of silver, 6000 pieces of gold, and ten sets of clothes (which were quite valuable in those days). Naaman has everything he needs, the backing of a powerful person, precious metals worth over $70,000 in today's economy, plus the clothes. He is ready to go, or so he thinks. The truth is he is off track already through his own arrogance and pride, which he will have to face in the days to come.

So Naaman takes off and makes another mistake, he goes to the wrong man. Back in Syria the woman did not say to go to the King of Israel, she said there was a prophet in Samaria. Not much has changed from then until now. People with addictions rarely follow directions, especially Christians. The struggle seems to be accepting that even though a person has knowledge of the Word of God, they are still sick. Christians who are covering up an addiction are sicker than most, the shame and guilt on top of the addiction leads to extreme measures to hide the problem. When a solution is finally desired, there is a "pre-determined expectation" of how God is going to solve the problem. Naaman had the same issue. Not only did he fail to follow directions, but he assumed that the cure could be purchased with enough money and influence. He had already determined how God was going to heal him, without any regard for the Lord's divine wisdom. Naaman was wrong, and so are people today who take the same approach. It lacks humility.

The King of Israel does not handle the situation well either. He could have easily said that he was not the right man for the job, but instead he tears his clothes, a sign of great distress and displeasure. Since God had already planned the outcome, He simply brings the prophet Elisha into the picture, the same one who the nameless woman back in Syria had referred Naaman to. Elisha sent a message to the King of Israel questioning why he was acting in such a way, and gives instruction for Naaman to be sent to him.

Today, we still have people in positions of authority that don't know how to handle addictions. They are not the right person, they do not know how to respond, and they do not know where to find help. These concerns are not based on a type of profession but on a lack of experience or knowledge. Christian clergy have received a bad reputation along these lines, due to *some* not understanding that they are not the right person to talk with. They are one dimensional, deliverance in a moment only. Christianity has an abundance of compassionate people, who have given their lives to God's work. Clergy from all types of backgrounds and denominations, many of whom either know how to respond to an addict, or know they're not qualified and use other resources. What makes the difference between effective clergy and misguided ones is truth. Some know the truth about addictions, others do not.

In the late 1990's, I attended a conference at the Marin Civic Center put on by Ross Hospital. The speakers were highly recognized in their fields, which included David E. Smith, founder of the Haight Ashbury Free Clinic in San Francisco, CA. At that time, Mr. Smith had already achieved long term experience dealing with addictions and treatment. At the conference, he made a statement about the Christian church, "the sleeping giant is waking up." His reference at that time was truth, the fact that the church as a huge body of faith was for the most part sleeping on the job when it came to addictions. While some may argue this point, it can't be ignored when it still exists today. Several times over the years, I have personally heard of churches that claim to not have "those kinds of problems." Years after that conference, I was speaking at a church about addictions. The next day a woman came to the pastor's office and complained "Why would you have a man like that speak in our church, we don't have those problems around here." The pastor responded, "what do you mean we don't have those problems, I just put a church member into treatment for addiction last week." A woman asleep in the pews, who needed to wake up to reality. It does still exist, and Mr. Smith was absolutely correct.

God has called people to various tasks within the body of Christ. Some to be clergy, others to support them. In Israel there was a king and a prophet. In this story, the king does not make good decisions or use the resources available to him, so God uses the prophet to guide the situation. Knowing where your limits are is a matter of wisdom and discernment. Anyone can apply this principle, not just clergy. Addictions can be complicated issues, different types of drugs and doses can have different effects. What is visible is often the least revealing of truth. All addicts lie. Christian addicts lie more. They have to. The truth is more agonizing when you know God and use drugs than if you don't know Him at all. Clergy that are not familiar with addictions should have a person they can trust who is familiar with them.

The king is asked to make a referral, and he does. It is hard to take this step, making a referral and moving over, but in many cases it's the right one. A recovering addict can easily pick up on the denial, excuses, and lies of another addict. Besides, it's not the end anyway, just the beginning, and there will be time for influence later.

Elisha requested for the man to come to him. It must have been quite a spectacle as Naaman arrives with chariots a blazing and goes to stand at the door of the prophet's house. His pre-determined expectation is about to take a major reality check. He was expecting the dramatic, an instantaneous event that would suddenly make his sickness disappear. He wanted to be delivered in a moment, just like today, many would like to be delivered instantly, especially Christians. But that did not happen. Elisha sends a messenger out to tell Naaman to go wash in the Jordan River seven times. Following directions was still a problem for Naaman. Instead of accepting the information, he gets mad. In fact, it was rage. It is at this point that we find out exactly what Naaman's expectation was. "*I thought that he would surely come out to me and stand and call on the name of the Lord his God, wave his hand over the spot and cure me of my leprosy.*" He had not only pre-determined the outcome, but also the process by which it would take place. He had it all figured out, but he was wrong. God's plan did not align with his, just as people today struggle to be free from addictions because they have already determined how God will deliver them. It seems that most of the time the expectation is for an instant experience, and why not, it's the easy way out.

A man we will call John E. #1 came to me and asked for help with an alcohol problem. He had been a Christian for many years, came from a good family, but turned to drinking at a young age and never stopped. Now in his forties, he was trying desperately to stop drinking and couldn't. He got involved with drugs at an early age, but by God's grace and deliverance had given those up long ago. Yet alcohol continued to be a problem. His story directly applies to Naaman's. Many a Sunday John E.#1 went to the altar after the sermon and prayed for God to take the problem away. Upon returning home he decided that nothing had changed, "guess it wasn't today" he would think, and then go ahead and get drunk. His pre-determined expectation was that one of these days God was going to do something in a moment. Maybe the minister, the man of God, was going to come over and call on the name of the Lord his God, wave his hand over the spot and cure him of his addiction.

Unfortunately, this approach had been learned in church by John E. #1 from sleepwalkers. After all, aren't there examples of God instantly delivering someone from an addiction? Do we not hear about and see testimonies of those who had this experience? And if God has all the power in the universe to deliver, and He delivered someone instantly, doesn't He just deliver all people the same way? The answer is no, not according to the Bible. There are examples of instant deliverance in the Bible just as there are examples of deliverance through a process. Naaman will eventually be delivered through a process, but at this point in the story he can not see it because he is blind to the truth, blinded by his own agenda.

So Naaman gets an intervention. His servants are aware of his problem, just as they are aware of what is taking place in his life. The common people in this story play some of the biggest roles, giving the correct information with nothing to gain. The nameless Israelite woman in Syria gained nothing, these servants gained nothing, and only one servant will try to gain something later and suffer for it. The words of Naaman's servants are wise as they make an appeal, *"if the prophet had told you to do some great thing, would you not have done it?"* Here we have some of the greatest wisdom of this story.

People seem to be ready to do something on a grand scale to solve an addiction problem, but will not follow simple instructions. Some want to travel great distances to go to expensive treatment programs, but will not go to a recovery support group for an hour for free. Maybe they saw an ad on television for a spa type treatment program by the beach and dream of how it's all going to occur. And if they do happen to go to a recovery meeting, there is a pre-determined expectation of how it is going to work. When that doesn't pan out well, they leave mad, blaming the program. There are servants in these programs who will provide the correct information with nothing to gain. What is needed from the addict is a willingness to follow directions. Naaman did become willing to follow directions, but not until after he entered the debate.

One common characteristic of an addict is their desire to debate. Wise in their own eyes they have it all figured out. But God's Word says in Proverbs 14:12 *"There is a way that seems right to a man, but in the end it leads to death."* Addictions lead to death, which is why debating over the solution is senseless. Naaman enters the debate when he delivers a grand dissertation about the quality of rivers in Syria being better than "all" the rivers of Israel. Really? Here we have a sick leper that has traveled a great distance to solve his problem, of which he is ready to pay huge sums of money, and he wants to debate over water quality. He's ready to take his ball and go home. The instructions were too simple. Recovery is a simple process for complicated people, and Christian addicts are complicated people who like to debate.

John E. #2 is a man I met personally, a Christian with an addiction to crack cocaine. While sleepwalkers will say this is impossible, it's hard to dismiss when John E. #2 confesses with all his heart that Jesus is his Savior, and still abuses drugs. I've personally met many like him. So why does he keep smoking crack? There could be several reasons, but his actions speak as loud as his words in revealing one of the problems. After spending a few years at a strictly faith based addiction program, and staying clean the whole time, John E. #2 relapsed with cocaine in just a few weeks after leaving. He came to our addiction support groups seeking help "after" relapsing.

Later that same night I received a phone call from John E. #2, stating his displeasure with a person using a foul word during the addiction group that night. He wanted to know what I thought about that, so I told him, "I think he should bring his friends." After a few of his attempts to debate the issue, I reminded him that ours was a ministry about helping people with problems, and we expect people to show up who have problems. That wasn't what he wanted to hear. Unfortunately, I also had to remind him that he needed a new testimony. His was a Christian in active addiction to crack. I recommended that he stop debating the small details and pay attention to the big problem, his addiction. John E. #2 had the same problems as Naaman, he couldn't follow directions, had a pre-determined expectation, and was a debater.

So how did Naaman get from rage to acceptance? The appeal of his servants plays a big role in another way. There was no pleading, begging, or bargaining; a defective approach that is used today by families trying to persuade an addict to get help. The servants gave an appeal that is worth studying. First, they came near and spoke to him. No arguing, yelling, shaming, or guilt trips. No promises for a good decision, just plain truth. They introduced common sense into the equation by pointing out his errors. Remember, the servants just saw what took place with the prophet Elisha and heard Naaman's comments about his expectations. They know what he wants; something on a grand scale. They appeal to him by pointing out that the prophet asked him to do something very simple. In other words, they speak common sense to his pride and ego.

Families can be as much a part of the problem as the addicts. They can also be part of the solution, unless they too want an instant, miraculous, pre-determined result based on their expectations. Sometimes families pour on the pity to help the addict, but that just makes them victims. It would have been easy for Naaman's servants to support him in a victim role, agreeing with the injustice of the prophet for being so offensive as to not come out and join the show. Instead, we get a solid example from Scripture for talking to addicts, from people who care enough to point in the right direction, even when it's not easy to hear. Today we call that tough love, and it works.

"When diseased sinners are content to do anything, to submit to anything, to part with anything, for a cure, then, and not till then, is there any hope for them." Commentary by Matthew Henry.

"Naaman thought he was such a great man that it would be an honor to come out to him, but Elisha thought differently. …The Lord not only wanted Naaman to learn a lesson in humility and obedience, He wanted men of all ages to learn God does not honor human greatness, and that His thoughts are not our thoughts, and His ways not as our ways (Isaiah 55:8-9)." Dake's Annotated Reference Bible: Pg. 672, 7th Prophecy a).

Whenever I'm talking to an addict, especially if they are under the influence of drugs or alcohol, I keep in mind that I am talking to a chemically altered version of the real person. I have used this to help parents deal with their children, especially adult children, encouraging them to remember their loved one minus the chemicals will be more like the child they raised. A young man about 20 years old was threatened by a good friend he grew up with, one who had developed a problem with alcohol. In a very ugly situation, this childhood friend physically threatened him while drunk, wanting to fight and not willing to let it go. Fortunately, there were other people who intervened. I encouraged this young man to consider that the man who wanted to fight him was a chemically altered version of his friend. We do not know for certain how Naaman's illness affected him, but we do know he had leprosy and was sick. It has to have influenced his thoughts and feelings, especially since he was a very successful warrior who obviously made good decisions under pressure. Yet here we find him as a valiant warrior who is whining like a little boy. "My rivers are better than your rivers." He was either a fake all along or his sickness had affected him deeply, and we now see an altered version as his sickness progressed. He will eventually prove the latter to be the truth.

Naaman has now accepted the solution, and is going to the Jordan to follow directions. After dipping seven times, his flesh is clean like that of a child. Naaman had to become like a child to experience God's grace, something Jesus told us we need to do (Matthew 19:13-14). There is a stark parallel here between being delivered through a process and recovery programs. Naaman was delivered through a process, one that was given to him by someone else. A simple process, not too hard yet highly effective. It didn't compromise his values or ask him to do something that would tarnish his reputation. Just follow directions, immerse yourself in the process, and experience healing. Seven dips or 12 steps, either way it's a simple process. The 12 steps are rooted in Scripture, which is a documented historical fact. Later in Chapter Six, we will take an in-depth look at this connection.

Then Naaman went back. The importance of this statement is understood in the fact that the distance between Elisha's house and the Jordan was about 30 miles, a three- day journey back then. He now stands before the prophet, the opposite of what he was expecting before. There he acknowledges the God of Israel as the only true God. Naaman then offers gifts to pay for his healing, but Elisha refuses, another parallel to recovery programs. The process of deliverance in recovery is shared free of charge. Sponsors do not get paid, they serve. When the basket is passed, if you have something you put it in, but it is not a requirement, it is a privilege.

Addiction treatment can get a bad name, sometimes deserved. For many, it is a chance to help people who are suffering, for others it's a way to gain wealth. People who are dying from addiction are confused enough, getting rich off them is hideous. It is not right to label all treatment programs as the same because they are not. Each must stand on its own merit and devotion to helping God's children. Some are good, others are not. We do not have to guess how God feels about it, Naaman's story tells us. Greed entered the heart of Gehazi, a servant of Elisha, and he decides that the prophet missed an opportunity to gain wealth. The story also reveals prejudice in the heart of Gehazi, by the way he points out the nationality of Naaman, an obvious judgment. And as if that wasn't enough, Gehazi brings God into his plan by saying "as surely as the Lord lives, I will…" As the story continues, so do the applications for us today.

Gehazi catches up with Naaman and continues his errors. He lies about being sent there by the prophet. After he gains some money and clothes, he heads back and tries to hide them from Elisha. Sin is progressive, it will always increase. Addiction over time always gets worse, never better. When the prophet questions his servant there are more lies and deception, until Elisha reveals the truth. The punishment for Gehazi is that Naaman's leprosy is now on him and his descendants. The transfer of sickness today may not be as literal as Naaman's leprosy going to Gehazi, but it happens nonetheless. Elisha spoke on behalf of God, as such we can see that God will deal harshly with those who take advantage of suffering people. And in case someone thinks it can go unnoticed, they forget that God sees everything just like Elisha saw Gehazi when he was in the middle of his deception, even though he wasn't physically in the same place. The mistake is when people seemingly get away with their selfish acts without consequence. Gehazi committed several sins before he was confronted and punished. People who take the path of getting rich off the sickness of others will pay a price in their own lives and their families, just like Gehazi did. Maybe not right away, as they live out lavish lifestyles, but it will happen. If a sparrow doesn't fall without God noticing, then taking advantage of His suffering children will not either.

The story of Naaman in II Kings provides a good example of deliverance through a process. It also has enough Biblical truths and parallels to recovery to show how our solutions today align with those of the Old Testament. Once Naaman was healed, he was clean when he finished the process. We have no other indication that his leprosy returned, so we are to believe that his deliverance was complete and lasting. While relapse into drug and alcohol abuse happens to some, it is not necessary. Entering recovery once and staying clean and sober is possible, and there are enough people who have this experience to support its validity. So what about the people who relapse. Theirs is a testimony of increased suffering. It happens to those who are delivered through a process, and those who are delivered in a moment. Both are covered extensively in the Bible.

Some who are delivered in a moment return to their sin.

Addiction is ugly, especially when a person has experienced the blessings of sobriety and relapses. Several scriptures give insight to describe how this occurs, as well as providing solutions for relapse prevention. *"For if they have escaped the corruptions of the world by knowing our Lord and Savior Jesus Christ and are again entangled in it and overcome, they are worse off in the end than they were in the beginning."* 1I Peter 2:20.

Some people use this scripture to debate as to whether or not the person was a Christian in the first place. Let the scholars debate, it seems obvious that knowing Jesus Christ as your Lord and Savior would make you a Christian. The real point here is that deliverance (escape) from the corruptions of this world applies to addictions. The King James Bible uses the word "pollution," something we can all relate to. When something created by God is at its best, it is clean. But when something enters from the outside that changes this condition for the worse, we call that pollution, which corrupts God's creation. Our bodies are temples of the Holy Spirit (I Corinthians 3:16). Addiction is a way to pollute the temple and cause corruption.

Eventually this portion of scripture quotes Proverbs 26:11, *"as a dog returns to its vomit."* It is a grotesque picture of a dog not only returning to its vomit, but eating it. That is what relapse looks like, a person not only returning to the pollution from which they escaped, but putting it back into their lives again. It is not a pretty picture.

Luke Chapter 11 gives an explanation of what happens to a person who relapses, as well as how to prevent it. Jesus is speaking to a crowd teaching them spiritual truth. In verses 24-26 He shifts to an explanation about evil spirits. *"When an evil spirit comes out of a man, it goes through arid places seeking rest and does not find it. Then it says, 'I will return to the house I left.' When it arrives, it finds the house swept clean and put in order. Then it goes and takes seven other spirits more wicked than itself, and they go in and live there. And the final condition of that man is worse than the first."*

This powerful story actually tells us what an evil spirit is thinking and saying to himself, before the fall of the person (relapse), "I will return to the house I left." Make no mistake; addiction is an evil influence ready at any time to return. People on all sides of the deliverance issue can learn from this insight. Deliverance does not guarantee permanent safety.

Addicts who are delivered in a moment or through a process can relapse, if they don't keep their guard up and act wisely. More about this will be covered in Chapter 4 discussing why "addicts must remember their past." There are examples everywhere of people who were delivered in a moment then relapsed, just as there are examples of people who stayed clean after an instant deliverance experience. The problem is that a person who was delivered in a moment has no answer for relapse, except to make the mistake of assuming a real conversion to Christianity never happened. But how is that even possible when an addict stays clean and sober for years, maybe even several years, then relapses? What was the source of their deliverance? From this we can say with confidence that a person who is delivered in a moment is still vulnerable to relapse, just as a person delivered through a process. The difference is not the method of deliverance, but the failure to fill their spiritual house.

Having a house swept clean and put in order sounds good, but it is not. What it really means for an addict is a "void." The problem of addiction was removed but nothing was put in its place. For the person delivered through a process, it means being active in a recovery program, and helping others who are struggling. The void is filled with recovery. For the person delivered in a moment, it means spiritual growth and replacing old ways with new ones. In either case the void needs to be filled, because evil is coming back.

One of the most tragic testimonies in Christianity is when those who are delivered in moment relapse. When they fall, they fall hard, especially if they've been put on a pedestal before the body of Christ, the church. It is dangerous to take a person who was recently delivered from addiction and parade them around as experts on how everyone else should recover. How do they suddenly know how the rest of the world should recover? And amazingly have the ability to pre-determine God's plan for others? We could call them Naamanites. They have it all figured out ahead of time. Giving a testimony to the grace of God entering a person's life and setting that person free from addiction is incredible, but God warned us about novices being put in leadership roles. I Timothy 3:6 gives instructions about qualifications of leaders in the church, which applies here also. *"He must not be a recent convert."*

What gives this issue such a volatile nature is the outcome, death and destruction. If we are going to serve God, then we must follow His instructions. The Bible tells us that our adversary has an agenda, to *"steal, kill, and destroy"* (John 10:10). When this happens to people whom God delivered in a moment, when their lives are tragically destroyed or ended, then we as the body of Christ must wake up to a solution that works. Talk with any missionary around the world and they can tell you of a person who was delivered from addiction, became a role model for the church, and fell. These people are so ashamed that they become isolated from Christianity, the exact opposite of what should take place. And while it is easy to blame the person, isn't the church responsible for setting up the circumstances, by elevating the person while they're still a novice?

God may have instantly taken away the desire to get high, but did he remove the sin nature also? Indeed not. And what about the Biblical processes of reconciliation and restitution, for all the damage that was done by the addict? This is where a process of deliverance has a clear path to staying clean and sober. The recovery process itself is a means of clearing the conscience. Being made whiter than snow does not equal being free of a sin nature. There is always work to be done from the inside out.

Jane E. #1 arrived at the County Detox facility sometime after midnight. She was extremely intoxicated and arrived with her boyfriend who was fed up, so he brought her to the door and said, "here, you deal with her." Having been treated like trash she was obviously upset and crying. It wasn't until starting the intake process that I recognized who she was. An athlete, runner of marathons, and by all worldly standards a very beautiful woman. Yet here she was, a total mess and unrecognizable. She stayed a few days and left. Not too long after I saw her out running, all dressed up in a colorful outfit looking as vibrant as could be. Anyone else would think she was a healthy person living the good life. But just a few days before she had returned to her own vomit, and would probably do so again. She never embraced the process of filling the void, she just ran away from her problems.

If we as the Christian community are going to be as effective as possible in helping people with addictions, then we need to concentrate less on the method of deliverance and more on the process of filling the void. Why? Because each person who is delivered has an evil spirit that is coming back, and if it finds the void it's looking for, it will return with seven other spirits "more wicked than itself." The progressive nature of addiction leads to death, and not all death is literal. Families die, so do marriages and other relationships. Opportunities go away, education is wasted, and spiritual gifts are ruined. Adam and Eve bought the same lie. Physical death is not the only type.

John E. #3 was a full blown addict in every sense of the word. He came to know Christ and was instantly delivered from his addiction. For seven years he not only stayed clean and sober, but was an aggressive and vibrant witness for Christ, a genuine "soul winner". At work, at home, anywhere John E. #3 was, someone was going to hear the Gospel of Jesus Christ. Then, distraction came in the form of a woman, and even though she drank alcohol, it was not a problem in his opinion due to the confidence of his sobriety and faith in Christ. His friends told him otherwise but to no avail.

John E. #3 took his first drink and began a downhill slide. His friends appealed, but he continued. Within one year, John E. #3 was dead. Alcohol related incidents, DUI's, and tragedy behind the wheel led to his decision to commit suicide. Whether John E. #3 is the exception or the rule matters not. He was a human being who was addicted. The evil spirit that left him never forgot, and waited for the right time to return with seven other spirits. We cannot afford as the body of Christ to assume we have addiction all figured out just because we know God. The consequences are fatal. We must strive together to do more, to gain wisdom and understanding, and be willing to change.

Those who fall back into the sin of addiction can do so as true Christians or those who never truly accepted Christ. It can happen to the just and the unjust. The fact is we do not know who is actually a Christian, only God knows as recorded in the Lamb's Book of Life. He doesn't show us the book, probably because we would separate and classify those we would help and not help. We just know they fall, and that's all we need to know.

Not all people who are delivered in a moment become Naamanites. There are those who are humble, grateful, and serve God, helping others without being proclaimed as experts. They embrace deliverance in a moment or through a process, because they're both Biblical. Yet we still find newly delivered people being generously funded to promote their deliverance as the only method of deliverance. They are put on pedestals by others in the church, and are more than happy to see their name being promoted, printed, and their testimony produced on video. The higher a person is raised on a pedestal the harder they can fall, whether delivered in a moment or a process. Some never get back up and hide in isolation. Recovery programs have a good solution for this problem, called anonymity. There are no celebrities in an anonymous program, just people helping people.

Let God choose who will be delivered by which method. Accept His divine plan for others, and focus on helping people find God's will for their lives, even when it's not the same as His plan for yours.

A Christian can be an Addict

Jane E. #3 gave her testimony one Sunday morning in church as a recovering alcoholic. Her pastor, church, and congregation supported her decision to give a testimony about how a recovery program had delivered her through a process. But upon finishing her story, a leader in her church went to the podium and said to the entire audience, "with a testimony like that you can't be a Christian." Having been deeply hurt by these comments, she was referred by a mutual friend to contact me for some scriptures that would help. Through e-mail, I wrote some comments about Naaman's story in II Kings, and reinforced the fact that a Christian can be an addict. The man in church was right in his own eyes, but blind to the truth. Proverbs 18:21 *"The power of life and death are in the tongue."* Jane E. #3 did not receive words of life for her testimony about being delivered from her struggle with alcohol. The man in church spoke words of death.

The Book of James is one of the main influences that shaped the original recovery program, Alcoholics Anonymous. One of the names being considered for A.A. during its forming was "The James Club," because of the influence of this book from the Bible. Today, if you visit the preserved home of the late

Dr. Bob Smith (Co-founder of A.A.) you will see a glass case in the living room. Sealed inside the case is a Bible, laid open to the first page of the book of James. According to the volunteer staff, Dr. Bob and his wife Ann read the Bible together all through Bob's drinking years. Their favorite book was James, and its influence is evident throughout the program of A.A. Dr. Bob was a Christian, and an alcoholic (addict). He was delivered through a process.

 "*What good is it brothers if a man has faith but has no deeds, can such a faith save him?*" James 2:14. There are several important principles to point out from this scripture. First, it's to Christians. Even though the name "Christian" was not used until later, the reference is to "brothers." It was being written to people who believed in Jesus Christ. Second, there is a reference to being saved from something. This is not referring to eternal life. While there are varying positions within Christian denominations about works and grace as they relate to eternal salvation, none of them apply here. This scripture is referring to a subject that is covered in James Chapter One: temptation. It is stating that a person can have all the faith in the world, but will not be saved from temptation without works.

 To understand this principle, we have to look at James 1:14, "*but each one is tempted when, by his own evil desire, he is dragged away and enticed.*" This scripture seems to give a picture of a person being grabbed and dragged away against their will, but this is not the case. The term "dragged away and enticed" is a hunter's term. It refers to prey being lured by using bait. We are tempted by our own evil desires, which lure us away from God and into the enticement of sin. Faith alone will not save us from the temptation; it must be accompanied by works. It is also worth noting that James Chapter One points out that being dragged away and enticed will ultimately lead to death. Addictions can cause a person, even a Christian, to leave their place of safety and pursue the high to the point of death. The bait Satan uses to destroy us is our own desires. He doesn't create anything, he never has, and he can only steal, kill, and destroy what has already been created. People are his favorite target.

To better understand this principle, we need to understand the hunter's term. The Pacific Ocean off the northern California coast is rich with aquatic life. Spear fishing and abalone diving are abundant along the Sonoma County coastline. While scuba tanks can be used to spearfish, it is illegal to use tanks for abalone diving, which can only be done through free diving (holding your breath). Abalone is a shell fish that clings to rocks on the bottom of the ocean, and is one of the more expensive fish to buy. For the person who dives for their own abalone but also wants to spearfish at the same time, free diving is the only option.

I have spent a lot of time over many years diving in these waters. During the times that I dove for abalone, I would also take my spear gun in hopes of finding the prize fish, a ling cod. These fish grow to be very big. In fact, they have to exceed the legal size just to keep. I was looking for one in the 30" to 40" range. The problem is that ling cods hide; they are a predator fish that normally hides in holes waiting for smaller fish to come by for lunch, literally. Some divers are skilled enough to hold their breath for long periods, allowing time to search through the rocky terrain. But the average free diver like me doesn't have enough time on the bottom to search around, so I developed another technique.

Taking the frozen trimmings from the previous dive's abalone, I would put them in a net bag and tie it to the dive float anchor line, about five feet off the bottom. It would then be placed in front of a hole or ledge in the rocks. The small fish would come by and try to nibble at the bag, and the hope was that a ling cod would come out of his hiding place and sit in the hole by the bag. This technique worked to spear ling cods in the 36" to 40" range on several occasions. As the hunter, I didn't pursue the prey. I lured him with bait.

The comparison is that lure of sin brings people out of their safety. We are tempted to leave God's protection by bait. The Bible says in I Corinthians 10:13 that He will provide a way of escape with every temptation. So why do Christians fail when it comes to the temptation of alcohol and drugs? Because they have all the faith in the world but no works to go with it. Some do not do anything until the temptation hits, then try to start "working" at fighting the temptation, not understanding they are already hooked. "*If a man has faith but no deeds, can such a faith save him?*" The answer is no, and according to James 2:26 "*As the body without the spirit is dead, so faith without works is dead.*" Those who do not die physically suffer in every other way.

We are safe as long as we are in God's will. Addicts will stay clean and sober by remaining in the will of God and working to help others who are suffering, not just living day to day feeling good about faith. Since God cannot tempt anyone (James 1:13), the temptation comes from our own desires. Satan knows that he needs to get us out of God's will, so he lures us with something we are "enticed" by. For the addict, this can certainly be drugs and alcohol, but it can also be money, relationships, material gain, etc. Sometimes he uses little fish to catch big fish, but either way he seeks to lure us into a vulnerable place where he can take a shot at us and control our choices. A ling cod with a spear in him does not have choices, it's too late. Sin has conceived, life and death are now the issues. Christians are subject to this very principle, denying it is delusional. Satan has to lure us outside of our hiding place, which is in the shadow of the wings of the Almighty. "*He that dwells in the secret place of the most High shall abide under the shadow of the Almighty.*" Psalm 91:1.

Satan seeks to entice Christians with bait so they will become subject to his attacks. It's the same old trick he has been using since the Garden of Eden, using the things we as humans desire to hurt us. We must have works to accompany faith. This is the most fundamental principle of addiction recovery, one addict helping another addict, one alcoholic helping another alcoholic. Even with people who are delivered in a moment, their best support system is people who have had similar experiences. When we are seeking to help other people based on our own struggles, then the power of faith and works work together, and will succeed in staying in God's will. Christians who think they can overcome the temptation of addiction by faith alone are wrong. So are those who think they cannot be an addict because they are a Christian. Both will learn the hard way that a violation of scripture results in hardship.

In 1998, God directed my path to focus on building a recovery ministry to help Christians with addictions. While I knew God was not calling me to help Christians only, He was directing me to focus on an area that definitely needed help. The first call I took was from Joe E. #4, a real eye opener. A middle age man, one who professed to be a Christian, was struggling with an addiction to cocaine. As we talked the conversation took an odd turn, he started asking questions trying to determine if I had the right kind of testimony to provide help for him. He had a pre-determined expectation from the telephone call.

His interrogation was really about establishing if I was a good enough Christian to give him advice. Several times he said, "how do you justify ... (blah, blah, blah)?" After trying for a while to answer his questions, I reached my limit. I reminded him that he was calling me to find help and suggested that he get a new testimony. He didn't understand so I explained. He was a Christian using cocaine, he needed to trade his testimony in for a new one. In other words, pride and ego were dominating his decisions. He was not listening, could not follow directions, and pre-determined the outcome. Joe E. #4 was a Naamanite. The basic problem was he could not accept that he was an addict as well as a Christian. Some calls I get today are from people who want sobriety but have a list of what they're not going to do to achieve it. I wonder why they call if they have it all figured out. It takes a lot of patience to deal with that kind of pride, talking to people who cannot follow directions but call and ask for it. This typically leads to asking the profound question, "how's that working for you?"

The plaguing question for Christian addicts is this "How can I know Jesus Christ as my Lord and Savior, and continue getting drunk or high?" I've had hundreds of discussions with people who are struggling with this question. Many have been told to "get saved," others encouraged to pray with more faith, and yet others are compared to an individual who was delivered instantly. Most people do not call a recovery program until they've exhausted all other options. Who wants to admit they are an addict? It's not on the list of career paths from the aptitude test in school. Many who have reached this point once had bright futures, which are now just a distant memory. Rarely do I get a call from a person who lacks faith, but most have a total lack of works to go with their faith. They want the man of God to call upon the name of the Lord, waive his hand over them, and deliver them from the addiction. According to the Bible, what's missing is works, and the biggest obstacle to accepting this is "contempt prior to investigation." Admitting to being an addict does not produce sobriety, it only makes it possible. Acceptance of truth is the first step to freedom, the rest is work.

A question I have asked occasionally on a group level is this: "How many of you prayed for God to remove your addiction?" Pretty much all the hands go up. Then I ask: "How many had that prayer answered?" In all the times I have asked this question, only one person raised their hand at the second question and he was very proud of himself. It's kind of a set up. People who are delivered in a moment do not need a recovery program. The ones who go to support groups are being delivered through a process.

Joe E. #5 met with me and a local pastor who knew him well. In the course of our discussion about his crack cocaine addiction, from which he had been two days clean, he began to tell us how the day before he was witnessing to a Muslim about Jesus. I asked Joe E. #5 if he told the Muslim the truth, which he happily affirmed that he had. Then I explained I was asking if he had told the Muslim that he is a Christian that smokes crack cocaine. I expressed my doubt that the Muslim would want to know his Jesus if the real truth was known. Joe E. #5's problem was not his faith, he was trying to impress the pastor and I that day. His problem was denial of the fact that he needed to work a recovery program and be delivered through a process. He was a Christian whose faith was failing because it was all he had, and according to James 2:26, it was dead.

At a large Christian convention, there was a workshop on the subject of addiction. An attending pastor with all sincerity asked the speaker, "If getting saved through Christ doesn't deliver you from addiction, then what are you saved from?" Surprised by the question I said, "Hell," which seemed like the obvious answer but was met with a moment of silence and strange looks. The issue in Christianity is attaching a pre-determined expectation to salvation through Jesus Christ. When it doesn't work for the addict, we are providing more guilt and shame to a person who already has plenty. Some people are delivered instantly from addiction when they receive salvation through Christ, but that doesn't mean it is the only way to be delivered. Some Christians are delivered through a process after trusting Christ as their Savior. Both had better understand the principle of works and faith if they want to stay clean and sober.

Romans 8:5-6 talks about a subject that applies to all people, and reinforces how a Christian can be an addict. It tells us that we have two parts to our mind, a carnal mind and a spiritual mind. According to the scripture, these two are at war with each other for control of a person. The carnal mind leads to death, the spiritual mind leads to life and peace. It's interesting that in the last 100 years, mental health has identified that the two physical sides of our brains have different functions. They have also identified that the addictive compulsion lives in one side and our spiritual connection to God in the other. What the apostle Paul wrote about 2,000 years ago was absolutely true. There is a war going on for control of the mind. When an addict relapses or uses, it starts with a thought to take the bait and leave their place of safety.

John 4:24 states that *"the truth will set you free."* It also might upset a person's denial. Acceptance of the truth is the first step to freedom. If we're going to personally know Christ as our Savior, then we have to accept the truth of being a sinner. We must confess, which means to agree, that we have a problem. The same applies to addiction. Any denial of truth, any lack of acceptance, will only lead us away from God.

Romans Chapter 7:18-25 give an accurate description of how an addict thinks and acts, including Christians. Paul wasn't writing this just to the spiritually lost, he was writing it to all of us. Probably no other scripture more accurately describes the struggle of an addict than Romans 7, especially for someone who relapses over and over again. A verse by verse breakdown will help make the connection, and keep in mind this is being applied to the person who wants to quit. Those who do not want to quit generally are not reading the Bible or any other book about the solution, they're not yet ready. Those who are getting high and reading the Bible or recovery books are generally the most miserable. Romans 7:15-26:

- *Verse 15 "I do not understand what I do. For what I want to do I do not do, but what I hate I do."* Addicts are confused. When they want to do what is right but find themselves doing wrong, they are miserable and no longer enjoying the high. Such is the strange mental twist of a person who is told they will die if they drink, and they drink anyway. Some try to get clean through self knowledge, but it doesn't work for addicts. Gaining insight is not the answer.

- *Verse 16 "And if I do what I do not want to do, I agree that the law is good."* When an addict is ready to get help, they will admit they cannot control the problem and agree that they cannot stop on their own. Those who still claim they can control the problem are not agreeing with the "law."

- *Verse 17 "As it is, it is no longer I myself who do it, but it is sin living in me."* A reference to the physical element of addiction which is covered in Chapter 3. There is a separation here between the sin and the person, made possible by becoming a Christian. Paul at this point was a Christian, and said something else was still living inside of him that was opposing his faith.

- *Verse 18 "For I know that good itself does not dwell in me, that is, in my sinful nature. For I have the desire to do what is good, but I cannot carry it out."* The desperation of a person who knows they have a problem but can not stop, unable to carry out even the right motivations. Just wanting to quit isn't enough, because even Christians cannot carry it out.

- *Verse 19 "For I do not do the good I want to do, but the evil I do not want to do—this I keep on doing."* The insanity of addiction; as a dog returns to its vomit.

- *Verse 20 "Now if I do what I do not want to do, it is no longer I who do it, but it is sin living in me that does it."* Restating the principle of verse 17, but adding the clarity that as a Christian we can and will do things that we do not want to do.

- *Verse 21 "So I find this law at work: Although I want to do good, evil is right there with me."* It is not a matter of will power or morals, it is a "law" of spiritual truth.

- *Verse 22 "For in my inner being, I delight in God's law."* People who do not know God will not delight in His law.
- *Verse 23 "… but I see another law at work in me, waging war against the law of my mind and making me a prisoner of the law of sin at work within me."* This is an accurate description of the internal struggle addicts experience; multiple issues at work within the person. Being a Christian makes this even more of a struggle than with non-Christians.
- *Verse 24 "What a wretched man I am! Who will rescue me from this body that is subject to death?"* No more denial, a wretched Christian… If that can be accepted, then the focus shifts to finding a solution by asking who is going to rescue this person.
- *Verse 25 "Thanks be to God, who delivers me through Jesus Christ our Lord."* This whole dialogue is written to Christians. Chapter Five will address how non-Christians find sobriety through the power of God. This verse also confirms that God will rescue the addict. Families who try to rescue them are playing God.
- *Verse 26 "So then, I myself in my mind am a slave to God's law, but in my sinful nature a slave to the law of sin."* The problem of addiction centers in the mind, according to the basic text of A.A. (the Big Book). They learned this principle from Christians and the Bible, confirmed by their own experiences through a combination of faith and works. An addict must submit to God's law, but always remember there is a "sin nature" waiting to take control, the "flesh." It is the physical element of addiction.

CHAPTER THREE

There is a Physical Element
of Addiction

Probably no other principle of addiction divides people and draws the battle lines more than this one. The physical aspect of addiction is referred to as the disease concept. Large Christian organizations reject this concept, including ones that identify themselves as addiction treatment programs. Whole denominations scoff at the idea that addiction could be a disease which are more examples of contempt prior to investigation. For the person dying of addiction in the pews, there is hope. *"When diseased sinners are content to do any thing, to submit to any thing, to part with any thing, for a cure, then, and not till then, is there any hope for them."* Commentary by Matthew Henry.

Just as Romans Chapter 7 gave insights as to the fact that a Christian can be an addict, it also is a good place to investigate the physical element of addiction. Beginning in verse 14, the Apostle Paul writes about a conflict from within, a struggle with knowing what to do but not doing it, and then not wanting to do something and doing it anyway. This is the war that an addict fights. It is really the lower percentage of people with addictions that do not want to stop. Christian addicts have an abundance of guilt and shame over their struggles. They want desperately to stop and know they need to, but continue doing the opposite.

After establishing this struggle, Paul writes in verse 17 that "… it is no longer I myself that do it, but it is sin living in me." He says in verse 21 "When I want to do good, evil is right there with me." Eventually Paul declares himself to be a "wretched man" who needs to be rescued from the "body of death." He thanks God who does this through Christ, and concludes to serve God with his mind while still serving the law of sin with his flesh.

Using these principles of Scripture, it is easy to see how Matthew Henry called us "diseased sinners" who need to surrender to God for hope. In doing so, he points to the physical element of sin, which Paul clearly stated was active within his flesh. A disease; a physical problem with a spiritual cure. The principles that support the disease concept of addiction are the same principles that support sin as a disease in every human being. The same problem with the same answer. The difference only lies in how God will work in an individual's life to provide the grace to overcome.

As discussed in the previous chapter, James Chapter 1 talks about the progression of sin. After establishing that a person is lured outside God's will by their own desires, verse 15 tells what will happen. "*Then, after desire has conceived, it gives birth to sin, and sin, when it is full grown, gives birth to death.*"

There is a physical element of sin being described that is the same as an addict taking drugs into his body, or an alcoholic drinking booze. The scenario is of a woman becoming pregnant and giving birth. When the seed enters from the outside, a human being is conceived, starts to grow and develop, and eventually the child comes out.

When we allow sin to enter our lives, we open ourselves to outside influences that come in and conceive with sin in our flesh. They grow and develop, eventually coming out into our lives. The difference here is a child brings life and sin brings death; none of which would have happened if the seed had not entered the body. The physical condition is always there, dormant but living, ready to be activated at any time by the entrance of just the right element. For everyone, when the Holy Spirit enters our heart we are "born again," a seed that brings life. But in the flesh, everyone is not affected by the same seed. Men do not get pregnant and non-alcoholics can drink. Yet, we all have at least one sin condition that is ready for a seed of death. For some it is alcohol and drugs. For others, it is sex, money, hate, pride, etc.

This is why the physical element of addiction is referred to as the disease concept. An alcoholic can stay sober as long as they do not take alcohol into their bodies. Once the alcohol enters, it conceives and changes the person. They will physically react to the entrance of alcohol, a condition that will grow and develop, and eventually cause death. Do not be fooled by the same lie Adam and Eve bought into, physical death is not the only type. Death to relationships, vocations, and families, children growing up without parents. Divorce, and single parents trying to clean up the mess left by the other person. Addictions cause more than physical death, just call it sin. But sin cannot control you until you are lured outside the will of God and allow it to "reign in your mortal bodies." Without doubt, there is a progression of sin that at some point becomes an issue of the flesh. There is a physical element of addiction. *"Therefore, do not let sin reign in your mortal body so that you obey its evil desire."* Romans 6:12.

Healing from the effects of sin is God's desire and Satan's opportunity for distraction. Christians need to fully understand what every advertising agency already knows. At a time when I was developing some ideas about addiction through personal studies, I made a business trip for the company I was working for. On one leg of the flight I found myself sitting next to an executive of an advertising agency. My studies had recently brought attention to the connection between addiction and advertising. It seemed to me that my work trying to help addicts recover was targeting the same issues within a person that advertisements were targeting.

Specifically, internal scars and pain which can be resolved through a process of recovery, were also being addressed by a product to make a person whole and feel better. All a person needs is to bring this item into their life and they can gain something of internal value. Ads that claimed to restore youth, give you what you've always wanted, or just provide what you deserve. Fantasy, lust, and delusion are common tools of advertising, as well as shame and a feeling of being less than. These are also common struggles for addicts. The vast majority of ads are based on fantasy, which the ad agencies know will make people buy products. It also seemed both the advertisers and I were addressing the brokenness of people, but for opposite reasons.

During the flight I asked the executive if we could talk frankly. I told him about the theories of recovery and advertising trying to connect with the same brokenness in people. His response has stuck with me for years. He asked this question, "What is your favorite soft drink?" I told him and he asked another question, "When did you start drinking that type/brand?" I answered that I started when I was a child. Then he said, "That's what we know." For me, his answer both confirmed and enhanced my question.

He was saying a couple of things. One, that ads target young people to gain customers for life. Two, that adults with unmet needs can also be targeted. Call it underdeveloped or immature, the scars and pains of life often stop the emotional growth of a person, which is why they turn to drugs and alcohol. A substance entering the physical body to solve an internal problem, which only creates more problems. Companies spend huge sums of money wanting you to believe that their product will be the seed that brings life. It is using pleasure for all the wrong reasons. Lured by bait, dragged away and enticed.

Trying to divert attention away from the flesh and split hairs over the word "disease" is futile. Even Webster's Dictionary describes a disease as "a condition that prevents the body or mind from working normally." Would Christians go to a doctor and debate the definition of a disease if it was ruining their lives? Or would they focus on the solution to the disease. Christian contempt for the disease concept is due to lack of investigation, a lack of truth. But what is worse than lack of wisdom is to have contempt for a solution that saves lives, one that is rooted in Scripture, and honors God. In my Bible these types of people are called Pharisees, and Jesus didn't have kind words for them.

Put aside any pre-determined idea you may have about the physical element of addiction, and follow the investigation.

Schools of Addiction:

There are mainly three Schools of Addiction that have a position on the subject of the physical element, the disease concept. These will be the focus of our investigation:

School 1 - Complete rejection.

School 2 - Acceptance of the physical element with rejection of the disease concept.

School 3 - Acceptance of both the physical element and the disease concept.

School 1 seems to believe that if addiction is a disease, then we have simply made excuses for people with these types of problems. Its pupils proclaim in a condescending tone, "what used to be called drunkenness is now called a disease." Or simply, "what is the world coming to?" These are subjective opinions based on partial information. Most people expressing them do so with righteous indignation. The problem is that School 1is attended by Christian addicts who cannot stay clean and sober and are suffering under the mistake of being misdiagnosed. Deliverance for them is like a mist in the wind. It comes for a time and vanishes quickly, if it comes at all.

The main issue with School 1 is using a specific word (addiction), then rejecting what it means. These programs are usually referred to as "faith based," which have a Biblical foundation without secular recovery groups or methods. But if they do not believe in the disease concept, then they should not use the word addiction, as the use of the word came from the development of the disease concept. How can a person reject the idea of the physical element of addiction by claiming it does not exist, then ask God to remove it? If School 1 is going to just call it sin, then just remove the word addiction from the curriculum and call it sin. Fortunately, some of the more effective Christian programs helping people with substance abuse and other problems in life have done just that, discontinued using the word addiction. Others that are still clinging to their right to be wrong should follow suit.

What confuses so many people is how organizations that aspire to the teaching of School 1are succeeding in helping "addicts" get off drugs and alcohol. Simply put, they are not addicts. The basic text of Alcoholics Anonymous (The Big Book) gives an accurate description of this principle. It states how there are basically three types of problem drinkers: the moderate, the heavy, and the true alcoholic. The first two suffer problems in life but have not acquired the physical disease; the third is an alcoholic because he or she has acquired the disease. The same is true for all addictions.

In some ways this ties back to Chapter 1, deliverance in a moment or through a process. People who are delivered in a moment do not need a treatment program. They have received deliverance already. They should, however, engage in a discipleship type program to *"grow in the grace and knowledge of our Lord and Savior Jesus Christ.*" II Peter 3:18. Others who God will deliver through a process need to seek Him to know which process. Some are addicts, others are not. Everyone does not need 12 Step recovery, just as everyone does not need to go to School 1.

Again, the main issue is the use of the word addiction. Let's say that you went to a doctor for a health need and the diagnosis you receive is based on the personal preference of the doctor. And consequently, the good doctor gives everyone the same diagnosis. Most people would quickly get a second opinion. Would you go to a dentist for a broken bone? Or a foot doctor if you were pregnant? This line of reasoning is easily recognized as absurd, yet this is exactly how some people speak about addiction. It is wrong when God delivers someone from addiction only to have that person become an expert on how everyone else should be delivered. And of course, it's the same way they were delivered.

The truth is there are people with all kinds of motives and programs working to help people with a variety of life's problems, especially those related to drug and alcohol abuse. Compassion should win out here, not pride. The consequence for an improper diagnosis is immense suffering, destruction, and death. We need to be more interested in helping someone find the right program according to God's will, and not the one we prefer just because it worked for us or it fits our preference for others.

Every program has testimonials of success stories, which should bring glory to God since He ultimately provides deliverance. It would be great to see deliverance of a suffering human being become paramount to the agenda of proving who has the right method. It is easy to believe that God would be pleased. There are so many people who have found deliverance in a moment through School 1 who could work together with the multitude of people who have been delivered through a process in School 3. Both sides would need the absence of pride, retirement of sea lawyers, and investigation prior to contempt to make it happen. But it is possible.

The second School of Addiction teaches the acceptance of the physical element of addiction while rejecting the disease concept. This is a complete contradiction because the physical craving and allergic reaction to alcohol/drugs is the disease. People who have struggled with addiction fully understand the craving and the reaction, but some have been taught to reject the idea that they might have a disease called addiction. This seems a bit trivial given the potential impact to the addict's life and the lives of their family and friends. School 2 is for those who want a solution but only want to accept the parts that make sense to them. They want recovery on their terms, and cannot see the confusion of a chemically altered mind trying to figure it all out. They like to participate in the debate, which, in light of the consequences, is pure insanity. Graduates of this school are the debaters who have the highest potential to speak words of death. Christians need to speak words of life.

Television ads provide a good view of this type of program. You can go to a treatment center that resembles Club Med. Complete with spas, massage therapy, and a host of other perks. You can be delivered permanently. School 2 probably helps the least amount of people. For one, it is just too specific as a solution. Second, the potential for a wrong diagnosis is huge. For most people it's just too good to be true, and for the delusion of an addict's mind, it's like offering candy to a baby.

During a visit I made to meet the staff of the local mental health provider, some discussion took place about referrals to treatment programs. A few staff members talked about a person coming into their facility and asking for placement in the program they saw on TV, the one by the beach with a promise of no longer being an addict. And, this person wanted the local mental health clinic to pay for it. The humor of this overshadows the tragedy. This person had accepted the need for change in their life, enough to take the difficult step of exposing themselves and asking for help, only to be mixed up with the notion that deliverance comes easy to those who have enough money.

Ultimately, School 2 is successful for those who have struggles in life that aren't too difficult. A moderate problem drinker perhaps, who wants to stop. It is their school's acceptance of the physical element by using the term addiction, while rejecting the idea that addiction is a disease that will hurt more people than it will help. Programs run by School 2 are typically people who are just in it for the money.

The third School of Addiction is for those who believe or want to learn about the physical element and the disease concept. Christian pupils of School 3 want to know if God's Word can mutually support these concepts. It really just takes a simple examination of the scriptures to understand the truth. School 3 is also for addicts who have tried Schools 1 and 2 unsuccessfully. There are also examples of people who have tried School 3 and failed multiple times, only to succeed in School 1. Hopefully when this happens, they do not become experts on addiction. Whether or not a person is delivered in a moment or through a process is not based on if they have the disease or not. It is based on how God responds to the problem.

II Corinthians 12:7-10 is a scripture best known for the apostle Paul's description of the "thorn in the flesh." This and several other principles found in this scripture support the physical element of addiction and the disease concept. There is plenty of commentary on the nature of this thorn with as many opinions about what it is, but the majority agree that it is literally a physical problem. After all, it is a thorn in the "flesh." Paul asked God three times to remove it, much like Christians today are asking God to remove their addiction. The Lord said no to Paul, and He can say no to people today according to His will, including Christians.

God chooses who will be delivered in a moment and who will be delivered through a process. He decides whose thorn will be removed and whose is not. Our pre-determined expectations will not change this truth. God is sovereign, He has each situation planned out, and has not relinquished this authority to any human being. Paul is not being held up as the only solution for all mankind, and the focus of his dialogue with God is really about the solution, which is grace. Far too often we see people who were delivered in a moment from an addiction being held up in front of the church or Christianity as the one and only way that God deals with this problem. The thorn in the flesh is a thorn in this mentality.

Review of Bible Commentaries regarding II Corinthians 12:7 Thorn in the flesh:

> *"Everyone who has become familiar with commentaries knows that almost every expositor has had his own opinion about this, and also that no one has been able to give any good reason for his own. Most of them have been fanciful; and many of them eminently ridiculous."* Commentary by Barnes.
> *"Though God accepts the prayer of faith, yet he does not always give what is asked for: just as he sometimes grants in wrath, so he sometimes denies in love. When God does not take away our troubles and temptations, yet, if he gives grace enough for us, we have no reason to complain. Grace indicates the goodwill of God towards us, and that is enough...."* Commentary by Matthew Henry (MHCC).
> *"...God will either work a deliverance for them speedily, or most assuredly support them in the trouble, as long as he is pleased to keep them in it."* Spurgeon Morning Evening (March 4 — Morning) 127.

A brief review of a few commentaries gives enough information to establish truth and move on to the application of the principle. Belaboring the issue of what the thorn represents is left to the debaters.

There's a persistent issue which exist between some churches, mostly those who adhere to the curriculum of School of Addiction 1, and recovery programs. The objection is typically phrased as "you shouldn't call yourself an addict." There seems to be some problem with identifying with your problems. So what do Christian sinners call themselves besides sinners? It gets a little more skewed when Christian recovery programs say not to call yourself an addict, but it's okay to be a "child of God saved by grace."

The scripture regarding the "thorn in the flesh" is good support for Christians and non-Christians alike who choose to call themselves alcoholics or addicts. The identification is a daily reminder that the thorn is still there. Complete abstinence is the only solution, and when a person calls themselves an addict, they are accepting this fact. Then the rest of the scripture can apply, glorying in the weakness so the power of Christ may rest upon them. Paul finishes by stating that when he is weak, then he is strong.

The necessity of the thorn for an addict or alcoholic is the acceptance that any drug or alcohol will trigger the craving in the physical body. For millions of people who God chose to deliver through a process, this thorn is the messenger to never drink or use again, not get too proud or too conceited, and never forget that addiction is just waiting to be enticed (James 1:14). For those who are delivered in a moment, there is the risk of relapse. Rejecting this truth has led many who were delivered through both methods back to their old lifestyles.

On one of the mission trips I took out of the country, there was an opportunity to work with several young addicts and their families. All of the young men and women had been actively using drugs and had all found recent deliverance through the church. Their pastor was advocating a recovery program because he had seen this quick deliverance turn ugly too many times before. The idea of working a recovery program did not sit well with the addicts. "Why should we do that? We've been delivered."

Within six months all but one had relapsed (the condition at the end was worse than the beginning). Several factors played into this situation, one was the complete rejection that a physical element, a thorn, remained with them after being delivered. Rejection until the craving was triggered, until the seed entered. I would say the majority of Christian addicts I meet struggle with this same issue. They cannot or will not accept the physical disease concept. The price for being wrong is tragic, especially when simple acceptance of the truth would set them free (John 4:24).

The focus of this scripture and its strong application to recovery programs lies more in Paul's response to God's rejection of his request. II Corinthians 12:9 states:

"My grace is sufficient for you: for my strength is made perfect in weakness. Most gladly, therefore, will I rather glory in my infirmities, that the power of Christ may rest on me."

Paul does not enter into a debate; he accepts his physical condition and turns to God's grace for a solution. He recognizes the fact that he can glory in his weaknesses, because by doing so the power of Christ will be upon him. He also talks about finding strength in being weak. Acceptance of powerlessness is the first step in recovery. It means admitting that an addicted person cannot stop using drugs and drinking by themselves, but with God's grace they can. The majority of the time this also involves other people, with rare exceptions such as someone sweating it out in a prison cell.

The physical element of addiction presents an interesting question, "How can a physical disease have a spiritual cure?" The answer is also found in Paul's response to God's refusal.

He acknowledges that his physical ailment will be addressed spiritually. In fact, Paul is so driven by God's rejection that he boldly states that he will take pleasure in all kinds of struggles in life, just so the power of Christ may be upon him. II Corinthians 12:10 states: *"That is why, for Christ's sake, I delight in weaknesses, in insults, in hardships, in persecutions, in difficulties. For when I am weak, then I am strong."*

Wow! Paul sees his physical problem as a catalyst to spiritual growth by which he will gain strength. In recovery this is called "an attitude of gratitude," being grateful for the addiction because it opens the door to understanding God's will and His Word.

"It was good for me to be afflicted so that I might learn your decrees. The law from your mouth is more precious to me than thousands of pieces of silver and gold." Psalm 119:71-72.

"Are you mourning over your own weakness? Take courage, for there must be a consciousness of weakness before the Lord will give you victory." Spurgeon Morning Evening (November 4 — Morning) 617.

A Christian addict who God delivers through a process should be grateful that their thorn was not removed. It provides the life changing urgency of such clichés as "one day at a time" or having "a daily reprieve" (Matthew 6). The truth is even those who were delivered in a moment should take the same attitude, because some go back to their sin as a dog returns to its vomit (II Peter 2:22).

Jane E. #4 is a woman who was delivered from alcoholism through a process of recovery. At the time she was celebrating about 25 years of sobriety, she was also struggling with losing weight. Having tried many diets, she decided to explore the possibility that her physical body was reacting to some type of foods that were triggering a craving. In order to do so she had to accept the possibility of having a food addiction, a physical element of her struggles. Through a process of elimination, she discovered that "flour" was the trigger for the addiction. If she ate anything made with flour, her body would react by craving food, any food.

Her ability to stop eating was much like the alcoholic who takes booze into his body and triggers a craving that can never be satisfied. Enough is never enough. Once she eliminated flour from her food, she not only discovered that she could be satisfied and stop craving food, but she also lost 80 pounds over the next several months and achieved a healthy weight. Her story provides two insights: there is a physical element of addiction, and deliverance from one addiction does not guarantee deliverance from all addictions. We are all delivered from something, but we are not delivered from all things.

Part of the problem with accepting the physical element of addiction is the misuse of the research. Certain groups of people have used the same principles to support poor choices in their lives, which has led the Christian community to throw the baby out with the bath water. Once addiction was identified as a disease, then gradually other issues became diseases too. People began claiming they too were "born this way," pointing to a genetic transfer of all kinds of issues. None of this removes the original truth, it just waters it down to where it is hard to tell the difference between real addictions and false ones. The disease concept does not pre-determine that anyone born into an addicted family will become and addict, they just have a higher risk.

In several scriptures God tells us that the "sins of the fathers and mothers will be passed on to the third and fourth generations." People who are born into a family with a high rate of alcoholism will have a higher chance of becoming an alcoholic. Yet, there are good people that come out of bad families. People who are born into a family that is void of addiction of any kind have a lower chance of becoming addicts. Yet, there are bad people who come out of good families.

When it comes to addiction, for every rule there's an exception.

So how do we apply the scriptures to understand what God is saying about the generational transfer of sin. Perhaps the best way is to focus on the generation that is not listed, the second. We are the second generation, the opportunity for change. If this was not true, then we would all have pre-determined outcomes in life. In order to really get this down we have to consider that we will receive from the first generation some degree of sin, or to use a recovery term, dysfunction. No one gets around this, we are imperfect people living in an imperfect world raising imperfect children.

Even if you were raised in James Dobson's home, you would still be a sinner raised by sinners. The delusion that the grass would have been greener somewhere else leads people to hopeless despair and asking "why me." Satan is the author of the "why" questions because they punish. The Bible also says that the blessings will be past down to the third and fourth generations. The change in direction from sins to blessings takes place in the second generation. Why is this so important to understanding the physical element of addiction? Because no matter what life has dealt us genetically, we can change.

A tremendous example of this came after several years of short term missions to Russia. We had the opportunity to help with a transition home for orphans. The home would provide a church run environment for children who were too old to stay at the orphanages. At that time, the age limit was 16. A statistic I was told in Russia was that 90% of the children in orphanages were there because of their parents' addictions. Another statistic was that within one year, 80% of the children leaving orphanages at age 16 were prostitutes, prisoners, addicts, or dead. The transition home was an effort to provide a chance for change.

After several years of the transition home helping orphans, something began to happen. The children were now becoming young adults. Those who moved out of the home stayed connected to the local Russian church who ran it. Love covers a multitude of sins, and these young Christians had no desire to stray into sin. Then, some decided to marry, and who better to understand life as a former orphan than another former orphan. Seeing beautiful pictures of wedding parties made up of all former orphans was heartwarming and emotional. But it was the next events that really blessed their lives, having children. The first time I saw a picture of two former orphans holding their child is when it hit me. The generational transfer of sin had been broken in one generation. Their children would not grow up as orphans. Change took place in the second generation because, despite all the imperfect influences, love prevailed. The choice was theirs, and God blessed them. The high risk factor was altered by choices. We all have the same opportunity.

Thus, the physical element of addiction is one factor that can be overcome. It does not need to be eliminated or removed to succeed. Denial of this fact only leads to relapse.

It helps to understand the relationship between the physical element and the generational transfer of sine if it's put into a mathematical formula.

There are three factors in our lives that sum up our risk of addiction:

G: genetic transfer based on birth;

I: influence(s) in life, includes nurturing and trauma (abuse, violence, etc.);

C: choices that are made individually; and

R: risk of addiction.

The math formula that puts these factors into a working calculation for the risk of addiction is:

$$(G + I) / C = R$$

(genetic + influence) / choices = risk

Most of us have little or no control over our genetic make-up and life's influences. Sometimes they just add up to a bad outcome. But we have a lot of control over the choices we make, especially when it comes to addiction. The only time this choice can be lost is *after* a person decides to consume alcohol or drugs. In other words, once the craving is triggered and the carnal mind is in control. For a person who truly desires to stay clean and sober, their choices are critical and are not subject to a pre-determined outcome.

In the math equation, these choices are applied by division, because our choices have more influence than our genes or experiences. If the value of the choices can be raised to meet or exceed the sum of the genetics and influences, then the risk goes down significantly. This is why some people succeed in recovery and others do not. Some people are still blaming their outcome on others and continue to make bad choices that lead to more suffering.

Since we cannot change the genetic makeup of who we are, we must decide how we are going to respond to it. Otherwise, our personal choices are taken away and we just become victims of another generation's sins. Examples of this are in the Old Testament when God judged Israel, but He also blessed them when they chose to seek His presence.

"If my people, who are called by my name, will humble themselves and pray and seek my face and turn from their wicked ways, then I will hear from heaven, and I will forgive their sin and will heal their land." II Chronicles 7:14.

No matter how great our choices, the risks are only minimized. For some people, the formula as it stands is enough. It's all they are seeking. They do not want God or any program just to stop drinking and using. These are people who quit without any type of program or treatment. But for Christians especially, it is not enough. God has to fit into the equation.

Mathematics have principles that remain constant, which includes solving for "X." When God chooses how He will act on a person's addiction, He applies the X factor. To show how this works in our equation all other factors are solved based on our human condition through addition, subtraction, and division. But God's factor is powerful, multiplication. For people who are delivered in a moment, God simply applies a "0" to the equation, which makes anything applied to the formula come out the same, "0." However, if God chose to deliver someone through a process, then He could also apply whichever factor He chooses, causing the equation to come out according to His will. No one advises the Divine Professor on this one. The choice is His.

$$(G + I) / C) X = R$$

(genetic + influence) / choices) * God = risk

    To keep the equation working properly, there has to be a few rules. All three original factors, genetics, influence, and choice have to be equal to or greater than 1, they cannot be zero. Only God has the ability in the X factor to apply a zero and nullify the other three factors. Also, God's ways are not like man's, so the greater His influence the lower the value of the X factor. Only a mustard seed's worth is needed. People on the other hand have to raise the value of their choices to achieve the best outcome, since we are still sinners.

    Take our choices, for example. Someone could say that doing nothing about the addiction amounts to zero, but that is not a true statement. Doing nothing is a choice. A decision to do nothing is still a decision. Even when people are addicted to drugs, they still have to make decisions. Just ask any family member or friend who has tried to make someone stop drinking or using. You can not make the decision for them; they have to make it for themselves. Often outside influences such as interventions, legal problems, or tough love by the family create the environment for good decisions, but it still comes down to an individual decision on the part of the addict.

    Even if the genetic and influence factors have been so bad that a high number exist on both, we can still make choices that will affect the outcome. The more good choices we make, the more the effect of the other two factors is reduced. Maybe we were abused as children, and the trauma led to addiction. Maybe we suffered a sudden traumatic event that turned our lives upside down. God doesn't have to erase those factors to apply His own. The catch is that God will not force himself into the equation. He must be invited through surrender and acceptance; we must choose His will over our own. It is our choice.

For a person who was raised in a family that has a multi-generational history of alcoholics, their genetic and influence factors will be high. If people see themselves as victims and fail to make good choices, the risk will remain high. But if a person is determined to have a better life and makes an abundance of good choices, the risk will go down, especially if they choose to invite God into their lives. The orphans in Russia had huge genetic and influence risks, but their high degree of good choices along with genuine relationships with God reduced their risk significantly.

So in this equation we find the answer that many Christian addicts are looking for. If a person already has a personal relationship with God, with Jesus Christ, how can they abuse alcohol or drugs? Using the math equation, the answer is easy to explain. God's factor has the most influence in the outcome of the equation, but our lack of making the right choices will drive the risk up dramatically. And if God will deal harshly with His chosen people (Israel) for making bad choices, then He will do the same with our choices. Christians who think their risk of addiction is gone while living in disobedience to God are living a lie. They will drink and use again. The testimonies are endless. One stands out above the rest.

John E. #3 is a Christian who struggled with both alcohol and drugs. In a discussion with him, I heard what had to be the most bizarre choice possible. He told me that at home in his refrigerator there was a six pack of beer sitting next to a chocolate bar. When I asked why, he explained that if he could eat the chocolate bar without drinking the beer that he was not an alcoholic. I told him "people that don't have a problem don't do things like that." I then suggested that he work a recovery program. As a man who spoke of personal faith in Jesus Christ as Lord and Savior, he was unable to stay sober because of his own choices and denial of the truth. And we all know what happened. He ate the chocolate bar first, then celebrated by drinking the beer. God was in his life, but was being nullified by decisions bordering on insanity.

One of the most influential testimonies I have heard came from an associate pastor's wife at a recovery conference, Jane E. #5. She told of growing up in horrible circumstances that included physical and sexual abuse. Her mother prostituted her for drugs. She was beaten regularly and suffered physically as a child beyond what most of us will ever know. She became an addict. Her story was heartbreaking, but so was her continued suffering by being taught through the church to forget about her past since she was now a Christian. (More about this in Chapter 4 – An Addict Must Remember their Past).

Her isolation was made worse by being a pastor's wife, unable for some time to be honest about her past. She struggled along until someone with the proper wisdom helped diagnose her with MPD (multiple personality disorder). Jane E. #5 made a critical choice, one that put immense value into the reduction of her risks. She accepted the diagnosis, mostly because she was tired of trying to live for God, while being dragged down by the influences from her childhood. I knew nothing about this condition other than watching the movie "Sybil" when I was young. What did catch my attention during her testimony was she would suddenly shift into another mode, either passive or aggressive. Her husband was there and explained that three of his wife's personalities had been present during the testimony.

In extreme circumstances it would take a lot of personal choices to reduce the risk of addiction. Certainly possible, but much, much more difficult. People who remain emotionally injured from trauma rarely make the right choices without solid interventions. It was not only applying the X factor that made the difference for Jane E. #5, but also understanding that God isn't limited to one number. Once she understood that God wasn't going to waive His hand over her and cure her disorders, she became free to experience change. Acceptance wasn't quitting, it just increased her choices.

I had the privilege of working with a Christian man who was a high school teacher. He had a computer lab that was so cutting edge that the local school district paid his program for their website management. The lab had a green screen, digital video equipment, and a sophisticated software program for full editing. It was incredible, and so was this teacher. After returning from the mission field in 2004, he helped our ministry produce a DVD presentation of the work we were doing in Russia.

It was while spending time with my friend editing the video that he told me about his upbringing, a severely alcoholic family. By every indicator he should have been an alcoholic. Genetically predisposed, influence growing up was not good, yet he chose to pursue a godly life and had a great family of his own, no pre-determined curses or outcomes. A good man that came from a bad family. A second generation success, because the God factor was multiplying his blessings.

Another young man came from a very prosperous home where money was not an issue. He had only one brother and they were a couple of years apart in age. The younger brother chose to go astray, getting into all sorts of trouble. The older brother pursued studies and a good career in financial management. Both brothers raised in the same home, genetic and influence factors the same, it was their choices that made the difference. And with God in his life the older brother prospered while the younger brother did not.

Even if a person had the exact information about the influence of addiction (genetically predisposed), what would they do with it? They would still have to solve the problem, not just live in it. Generational transfer of sin is a reality, but not based purely on genetics. However, there are issues related to the genetic factor that are covered in the Bible.

Polluting the Temple:

"Do you not know that your bodies are temples of the Holy Spirit, who is in you, whom you have received from God? You are not your own; you were bought at a price. Therefore, honor God with your bodies." I Corinthians 6:19-20.

Putting enough toxic substances into the temple will cause irreversible damage, unless by divine choice the toxic condition is reversed. Can a person with a disease be made clean according to the scriptures? Some people mistakenly assume that because the answer was yes for them it has to be yes for all. God can and does heal who He wants to, regardless of what denomination a person attends. All people can receive the promises from scripture of being cleaned inside, but this does not mean that all physical elements of addiction will be removed in every case. Paul's thorn was not removed, but sometimes we hear testimonies where someone's "thorn" was removed.

There is a lot of misinformation in the church on this issue. God is amazing, powerful, and gracious, but He does not ask any man how to accomplish His will in another man's life. We do well just to understand what His will is for our lives. Debaters try to be God's right hand man, but He already has one.

There is a side note from this scripture to visit briefly. If our bodies are temples of the Holy Spirit, then we should not engage in activities that will pollute the temple. Young people today are increasingly claiming the right to smoke marijuana, including Christian kids. Despite the fact that research shows excess marijuana use has long term effects, young people are ignoring the facts and believing people who stand to gain financially from legalized marijuana. From a Biblical position this is pollution of the temple.

A mom asked me for some advice with her son who was claiming to experience "manifestation of the Holy Spirit" while using marijuana. He was using this as justification for getting high. She shared a communication where he explained how it all worked and claimed this was his spiritual journey. In responding to the mother, I used in part I Corinthians 6:19-20 and talked about keeping the temple clean. The only thing this young man was manifesting was denial of the truth. A gross manipulation of scripture, but really no surprise. It was coming from a chemically altered version of her son.

In an article from December 2013, Nora D. Volkow M.D., Director of NIDA, made some revealing statements about marijuana use: *"It is important to remember that over the past two decades, levels of THC – the main psychoactive ingredient in marijuana – have gone up a great deal, from 3.75 percent in 1995 to an average of 15 percent in today's marijuana cigarettes. Daily use today can have stronger effects on a developing teen brain than it did 10 or 20 years ago."*

"Teens deserve to grow up in an environment where they are prepared to meet the challenges of the 21st century, and drug use never factors into that equation." Gil Kerlikowske, Director of National Drug Control Policy.

Young people, including Christians, need to know the truth. There is a physical element of addiction.

Addicts Must Remember their Past

The idea of remembering the past is the next most controversial Christian issue of recovery, second only to the physical element. But the impact of understanding critical truth is far more important than knowing about a disease. Lack of knowledge is one thing, but setting yourself up for failure on a life or death issue is quite another. Addicts must remember their past for two main reasons: 1) it's the most powerful tool they have in helping others who struggle with addiction, and 2) addicts who forget their past will repeat it.

There are a few scriptures primarily used for the idea that addicts must forget their past. These are mostly taught in School of Addiction 1, commonly faith based programs. Thank God for deliverance in a moment to those who succeed in School 1, instead of dying of a drug overdose or a drunken accident. Christians should collectively rejoice when a sinner is set free. But to use it as a means to teach the wrong solution to those God will deliver through a process is wrong. This is another reason why School 1 is attended by Christian addicts who can not stay clean and sober. They are not only trying to do something they cannot, but it is also something they should not be trying in the first place. Teaching confusion to people over a life and death issue is unacceptable. Christians need to know the truth about remembering the past, because addicts must remember theirs.

As mentioned in Chapter 3, the success of School 1 with helping people who have drug and alcohol problems is due to the fact that graduates of this school are not addicts, even if they use the term. They have problems, sometimes severe problems with substance abuse, but the reason they can successfully apply the teaching to forget their past is because they are not addicts. A person can apply this philosophy when it doesn't risk their life. Addicts can not afford that risk.

Proper understanding of the School 1 curriculum is important, since there are good campuses in this school that are not trying to teach people to literally forget everything in their past. Students who have graduated from School 1, those who have gained maturity over literal interpretations, will have the ability to apply the true Biblical teaching of forgetting the past. They understand how to use the memory God gave them without being controlled by past sins. Dropouts and freshmen of School 1 are quick to think that absolute forgetting is the goal, since they are not spiritually mature enough to see the impossibility. They are still influenced by the thinking of others, those who don't really understand addiction in the first place.

School of Addiction 2 takes the same position on this subject at School 1, but the curriculum never matures beyond infancy. They teach that success is achieved by never, ever, talking about the past. After all, who wouldn't want to forget the past with such promises of how a Club Med treatment program will change your life forever, for the right price. Such promises of grandeur. But School 2 is kind of like winning the lottery, huge promises with far more losers than winners. Trying to literally forget the past just leads to more confusion and contempt.

There is a connection between this recovery principle and Chapter One about how someone is delivered. Just like it is wrong for a person delivered in a moment to become an instant expert on addiction, it is wrong for the same people to claim everyone needs to face their past the same way they did. There are at least two distinct applications of this principle from scripture, not just one. Some can forget their past; others have to remember it. Those who sit in their own corner of success and criticize the other side are most likely freshmen of either School 1 or 3, those who need to continue their studies.

Contempt prior to investigation is like being a career student who never graduates and loses sight of the goal, which is to help suffering people. Anyone can be a critic, and the negative voice is always loud. There is really no room for pride in any addiction program, but it creeps into some and causes problems. It happens when one program claims to be the "right" answer for all people. Only one Jesus, only one Lord, only one way to stay clean and sober. Two out of three isn't bad, but it is. It's not good enough.

A skit was developed and filmed that has tremendous insight on addiction. It portrays why the right solution for the right person is absolutely necessary, and how trying to mix the students of Schools 1 and 3 can be harmful to suffering people, proper recruiting is essential. The skit was made by Mad TV, of all groups. It's called "Stop It," and stars Bob Newhart as a therapist (Dr. Switzer) meeting with a client named Katherine Bigman. It is six minutes of pure truth and has become a classic.

In the skit Katherine comes to Dr. Switzer for help with a problem. She is afraid of something that is controlling her life and needs help. Her character is one of uncertainty and confusion. Dr. Switzer explains his conditions for counseling that are unusual and self-focused. After some brief dialogue and humorous comments on both sides, he delivers his seemingly standard solution, just "Stop It." It doesn't make sense to

Katherine but it is all the doctor has for advice. As the skit goes on, Katherine reveals her other issues which show that she is a very sick person with multiple problems. Dr. Switzer continues to offer his one dimensional advice until he finally decides to offer another solution, which just turns out to be a more abusive version of the first one.

The content of the video has deep emotional and intellectual meanings, but it also contains simple truth. Applying these to the subject of addiction will lead to an understanding that "one size fits all" doesn't work. Just because a person comes in contact with one school or the other doesn't mean they have found the right solution. And while "Stop It" might work for some people, especially those who are not addicts, it might mean destruction and death to those who are. As Christians, helping suffering people find the right solution for them according to God's will should be our goal, especially for drug and alcohol problems.

So even students of School 1 have to be careful with how they apply the Bible. Going to extremes with one or two scriptures will lead to more graduates like Dr. Switzer, out in the world practicing insanity. These are the ones who should just "stop it," because they're causing more harm than good. Those who are delivered in a moment need to stay humble, and remember that it was God who chose their method of deliverance.

What about those who attend School of Addiction 3, those who God chose to deliver through a process? For them, any pre-determined expectation of forgetting about the past is futile and destructive. Remembering the past is one of the best tools an addict has to prevent relapse. This principle of addiction recovery came from several portions of the Bible which will be reviewed throughout this chapter. Before getting to those, a review of a few common School 1 scriptures is necessary.

"Brothers, I do not consider myself yet to have taken hold of it. But one thing I do; forgetting what is behind and

straining for what is ahead, I press on toward the goal to win the prize for which God has called me heavenward in Christ Jesus." *Philippians 3:13-14.* Paul uses the picture of a runner in a race, one who doesn't look back but presses towards the finish line to "win the prize." In fact, the part of the race Paul is writing about is the finish, that moment when the runner "leans in," pressing on toward the goal of winning. That is why the runner is straining, wanting to finish well and win the prize. This can be witnessed in any track and field event where a ribbon or electronic finish line is used, especially in a sprint or dash. Right at the end the runner leans into the finish line, pushing to the finish. Paul describes this as a lifestyle, one motivated to keep moving, knowing that the finish line is heaven. The runner doesn't have to forget the rest of the race to win, he just has to keep going forward and finish strong.

The importance of this principle was played out at the 2014 Winter Olympics in Sochi, Russia. A Norwegian cross country skier named Emil Hegle Svendsen had the lead in the 15-kilometer race. Coming to the finish he stopped "pressing" toward the goal and started celebrating prematurely. The second place skier from France, however, pressed even harder and turned the race into a photo finish. Svendsen did win, but by a fraction of a second. His decision to coast across the line with his hands up in victory was a poor choice. He won the gold, barely, with a finish where the quality of his race was overshadowed by the way he finished. This is what Paul is writing about.

Only God knows how many Christians have stopped pressing toward the goal and are coasting into heaven. By their faith in Christ they will win the prize, but not the way Paul is describing. They will make poor decisions which will overshadow their good life. Looking back is not the only way to lose focus, but it is the one Paul writes about as a warning. God wants us to know the pitfalls of not finishing well, of becoming complacent, or focusing too much on the blessings or failures of yesterday. The point that is made here is to keep going, keep pressing, do not quit while the race is still under way. It is not a call for Christians to forget all of their past, which by the way is impossible.

"The not yet state of Christian perfection destroys complacency and demands strenuous pursuit.

"...forgetting what is behind. The past accomplishments of his Christian career, which might induce self-satisfaction and a slackening of pace." Wycliffe Bible Commentary on Philippians 3:13-14.

Could you imagine trying to apply this scripture so literally in our lives? How does a person completely forget the past? That college education you just got? Forget it. Law school? Forget it. The promises you made at the altar of marriage? Forget them. Mistakes that you could learn from, forget those too. It's so hard to understand how anyone could come up with such a broad sweeping agenda based on one scripture, no, part of one scripture. It seems the agenda is driving the interpretation. Some rivals of School 3 take this position just because they are fans of School 1, not really understanding the application or the principle. They are like Monday morning quarterbacks, experts on things they have no experience with, or using their experience to be self-appointed experts.

This brings up a very important question. How does a person experience freedom from addictions when they are told to do something they cannot do? Such as female victims of sexual abuse who become Christians and are told to forget their past. This only increases the pain and continues the struggle of feeling flawed and different from everyone else, especially when they cannot forget. WWJD, speak life. *"Death and life are in the power of the tongue."* Proverbs 18:2. No one should have a pre-determined expectation of how God will deliver a person from their sin, suffering, and pain. There are similarities in the ways God delivers people, and there are also differences. Some people need to remember their past to experience healing, and victims of abuse quite often become addicts.

The Lord's continual command to Israel was to "remember." One thing God wanted them to remember was Egypt, when they were in bondage in the past. Addictions enslave people to the influence of the high, a bondage so gripping that people will die in pursuit of it. When God delivers an addict and sets them free, He wants them to remember where they came from, to remember their "Egypt." Several times in the New Testament, Egypt is referred to when someone is telling the story of how God delivered his people. He obviously wants us to remember what we were delivered from.

The application of Philippians 3:13-14 for addicts is to live above past failures, not in denial of them. Asking an addict to forget their past is a set up for failure. The main reason is those who are delivered through a process must, without question, embrace the Biblical teaching of reconciliation. They must forgive as they need to be forgiven for the pain and suffering brought into the lives of others by their addictive behavior. Forgetting what is behind for them means there is hope for the future, they won't have to repeat the past and can stay clean and sober. A person cannot finish the race like a champion if they continually focus on pre-race failures, looking back instead of leaning in. But an addict can run for the gold and remember their past, even talk about it regularly. The power of recovery is in our testimonies of the past. Satan's agenda is to fool addicts into trying to run from their past, because even he knows it's a path to failure in addiction. Overcoming evil is a matter of properly applying Biblical truth. *"They overcame him by the blood of the Lamb and by the word of their testimony."* Revelation 12:11.

I have personally spoke with many addicts who said, "but you don't know what I've done?" Their past was keeping them from pressing toward the goal of experiencing God's grace, forgiveness, and deliverance. Telling them to "forget it" is not the answer; about the equivalent of "Stop It." In those situations, the greatest asset I have is my past. When I am able to personally tell the horrible things I did and how God has loved and forgiven me, then hope is transferred from one addict to another.

One Sunday while coming into church I saw John E. #6, a man that I knew from around town who was struggling with drugs. He had come to church for the first time. He was tired and wanted to stop, but had a long history of alcohol and drug abuse. When I saw him in the Narthex, I went over, shook his hand, and asked him if he wanted to sit together in church. But he did not want to go in the Sanctuary, and explained how I didn't know what he has done. Just what Satan wants, a soul so close to surrendering to God but weighed down by his past, unable to go forward and find hope. I whispered in his ear the quick version of one of the most despicable things I did while using drugs. When I finished he looked at me wide eyed and confused, seems I didn't look like the kind of guy who would do such a thing. I told him that if God could forgive me then He could forgive him, and we walked into the Sanctuary together. An addict's past is the most powerful tool available in helping others. It cannot be ignored. John E. #6 didn't need to forget his past; he just needed to stop living in his failures.

When it gets down to the truth about the philosophy of School 1 and 3 on forgetting the past, the gap isn't really that big. School 1 doesn't really teach absolute forgetting of the past even if some pupils claim so, such as forgetting everything that ever happened. Some rebel campuses try to push a dysfunctional curriculum, but they do not represent the whole. Mature graduates of School 1 are not trying to forget everything they learned in life, just choosing to bury the dead bones and not talk about them. It works because they are not addicts. School 3 teaches to rise above past failures, but instead of burying the bones they just put them away until there is a purpose for bringing them back out. This works because they are addicts, and understand God's divine purpose in remembering their past. School 3 teaches its students how to bring the past into the present without causing harm to themselves or others, and it's based on Biblical teachings that will be covered later in this chapter.

When God called me into the ministry, I was not happy. After about 10 years of being delivered from drugs and alcohol through a recovery process, I had reached the point of coasting through Christianity. I was a game director in AWANA for several years, served as a deacon, and had a previous calling into the ministry that didn't seem to be going anywhere. Several years before God had called me into the ministry as a full time vocation, but I was lost in the process of how to get there. Success in my service to God was reassuring that he was blessing my life; His grace keeping me clean and sober was solid affirmation.

One Sunday night I went to church and an evangelist was speaking, Tom Shui. He was giving a message I had heard him give once before, "The God of the Second Chance," talking about the story of Jonah from the Bible. In the story God tells Jonah to go to Nineveh, but he heads for Tarshish until the Lord steps in and changes Jonah's direction. Jonah surrenders to God and follows the divine plan for his life.

Besides the message and the speaker, there was nothing the same that night. From the time I sat down God had my full attention, then Tom said the word "Go." It was as if it echoed through the sanctuary and certainly penetrated my soul. I knew exactly what God was saying, He wanted me to "go" into the ministry full time, and this was the second time He had told me. I had been real busy for Him, but had gone to Tarshish instead of Ninevah. It was time to change directions.

Not wanting to repeat my mistakes, I asked to talk with my pastor that week. As we talked about the recent events, he caught something I was saying and spoke the words I needed to hear, "If you live in your failures, you'll have to repeat them." Those words hit me hard, it was true. Even though I had reconciled much of my past through recovery and had remained clean and sober, I was bogged down by failures after becoming a Christian. It would take complete surrender for the direction of my life to experience God's calling. Another point of complete acceptance of God's will in place of my own. It's easy to lose focus on the way to heaven, which leads to coasting instead of pressing.

Pupils of School 1 might be quick to say, "that's why you have to forget your past, it keeps you from experiencing all that God wants you to be." The problem with that kind of thinking is that my experience with John E. #6 in the Narthex took place between the first and second call to ministry. I was using my past as a valuable asset at the same time other issues of the past were dragging me down. Maybe the "forget your past" principle isn't so black and white. Perhaps more investigation is needed so people can personally apply the scripture in both types of circumstances.

Another familiar scripture used widely by School of Addiction 1 is II Corinthians 5:17: *"If anyone is in Christ he is a new creation; the old is gone, the new has come."*

School 1 has multiple uses of this scripture, primarily to support the idea that an addict should not identify themselves as an addict. It is also used to reinforce the idea of forgetting the past. Once again we have contempt. School 1 staff and students should be able to refrain from calling themselves addicts without expecting the rest of the world to do the same.

This scripture is also commonly used by Schools 1 and 2 to reject the curriculum used by School 3. It seems as literal as forgetting your past that "the old is gone." Most often the first part of the scripture is quoted as "You're a new creation in Christ." Then the add on, "so you shouldn't call yourself an addict," or some other comment. Interpreting this scripture should take into account the very next verse, II Corinthians 5:18: *"All this is from God, who reconciled us to himself through Christ and gave us the ministry of reconciliation."*

Think about the concept of having an individual ministry of reconciliation. It cannot be about the future because it hasn't happened yet. Nor can it be about the present. Even if something was done a minute ago, it is now in the past. So a new creation in Christ has a ministry of reconciliation, *of the past.* What a tremendous truth from scripture, to know that we have a personal responsibility to clean up our past through the process of reconciliation. There is another word used in the Bible that has the same application, restitution. If our past decisions placed us in a position where we owe a debt, then we need to pay. The process of recovery demands both of these principles, of reconciliation and restitution, because misapplying them is death to an addict.

In a letter to Timothy, Paul gave some instructions that reinforce the importance of these two principles: *"...holding on to faith and a good conscience. Some have rejected these and so have shipwrecked their faith."* I Timothy 1:19.

If you want to understand addiction recovery, then you have to embrace the principle taught in I Timothy 1:19. It explains why people habitually relapse, and why some people fail in recovery programs even though they are actively participating. It answers some of the more commonly asked questions that non-addicts ask about addictions. Simple, but profound.

The main goal of recovery is to have a clear conscience, one that is void of guilt before God and other people. When addicts get clean and sober but resist the process of obtaining a clear conscience, they relapse. A shipwreck, that's what relapse looks like. To do this deliberately to one's faith is absurd, but it happens when the conscience is still stained with sin. The Bible promises that God will wash us "whiter than snow" (Psalm 51:7). Just as Naaman in Chapter One was made clean through a process, so the conscience of an addict is made clean through the process of recovery. The principles of reconciliation and restitution are a key part of this process, without which there is no recovery. Thank God that those who must remember their past have a process to be delivered from addiction, one that should not be diminished by those who were delivered in a moment.

Jesus even taught this principle in the Sermon on the Mount. He told the crowd *"Therefore, if you are offering your gift at the altar and there remember that your brother has something against you, leave your gift in front of the altar. First go and be reconciled to your brother; then come and offer your gift."* Matthew 5:23-24.

The subject of reconciliation was so critical to Jesus that he said it was more important than making an offering to God. The importance of a clear conscience cannot be understated. Going to people we have harmed and making things right is difficult. It goes against our sinful nature, our natural instincts. But with the power of Christ comes the opportunity we would otherwise avoid. We are told in the Bible that the "natural man" is against God, that his mind is at war with God's way of life. A new creation in Christ is no longer driven by their nature, but by God's Spirit. At that point, the new creation has *opportunity*, but still must take the action. Reconciliation with God has taken place, but reconciliation with other people has not. This scripture is about the past, because if you are at the altar and "remember," then you have a responsibility to take action.

Having addressed the philosophies connected to Philippians 3 and II Corinthians 5, there are some other scriptures that speak wisdom to addicts who are pupils of School 3. Learning and applying these principles can and will save an addict's life. They contain not only ominous warnings, but also understanding about life that we would otherwise never know. One of these tells us what evil spirits are up to. This scripture was covered in Chapter One regarding deliverance and some returning to their sin. Here, we will take a more in depth look and how it applies to remembering the past.

"When an evil spirit comes out of a man, it goes through arid places seeking rest and does not find it. Then it says,' I will return to the house I left.' When it arrives, it finds the house swept clean and put in order. Then it goes and takes seven other

spirits more wicked than itself, and they go in and live there. And the final condition of that man is worse than the first." Luke 11:24-26.

The description of an evil spirit coming out of a man is a reference that applies to all humans, male and female, and most certainly describes what happens when an addiction stops controlling a person's life. In other words, they "get clean and sober." The transformation that takes place is amazing. It's the bright spot of recovery programs. This is why it's so tragic when a person goes back to drinking and using drugs, especially after getting a glimpse of the good life. Why would someone trade the grace of God for getting high or drunk? And when they are asked why, the explanation never makes sense in light of the consequences. It is a common characteristic of addicts to not know why they relapsed. "I don't know why" is the most common response, and the most truthful. There are ways to prevent relapse and the scripture in Luke 11 tells us how.

The first thing an addict needs to understand is that the evil spirit which left is coming back, the same one. People who struggle with alcohol are not tempted with heroin. The evil that left is the same evil that will return. These demons do not call to schedule an appointment either, they just show up. Notice how the scripture says that it's out wandering when it has a thought to go back. That means there is time for something to take place in the addict's life, whether treatment or recovery. But when it arrives and finds the house swept clean, the evil spirit makes a plan. A clean house is not good in this case, it represents a void, something is gone but nothing came in to take its place. We know this because the evil spirit is pleased with what it finds, and wants to share it with other evil spirits because there's plenty of room. The house is empty. *"The house is swept, but it is not washed; the heart is not made holy. Sweeping takes off only the loose dirt, while the sin that besets the sinner, the beloved sin, is untouched."* Matthew Henry CC.

Then it goes again. Here is the second opportunity for the addict to take action. The truth is relapse doesn't just happen without warning; it is a process with a preventable outcome. Staying clean and sober in a recovery program requires some simple actions. If the addict follows directions from more experienced pupils in School 3, the house will be full when the evil spirit comes back and the rest of the scripture will not apply. But if the freshman sets their own agenda, has it all figured out through pre-determined expectations, then nothing good is going to happen. Eventually the "*final condition of that man is worse than the first,*" because the evil spirit is coming back with more evil than when it left. The scripture says they "*go in and live there,*" sounds like they just bust the door down and let themselves in. That's why addicts say "I don't know why." Even though it was preventable, they never saw the force of evil coming and relapse seemed like a spur of the moment event.

So how does an addict use this scripture to prevent relapse? First, take the warning seriously. The desire to drink and use will return, it's not a matter of if, just when. What an addict does between the start of sobriety and the return of evil will determine the outcome. Relapse is absolutely preventable, but testimonies have proven that any lack of diligence by the addict in working a recovery program will cause failure. It is not about perfection; it is just respect for the serious nature of the problem. The Bible tells us that Satan's agenda is to steal, kill, and destroy, but God wants us to have life, and to have it abundantly (John 10:10).

A recovery program has a few simple components, but they are not easy for an addict. Go to meetings, read the book, work the steps, help other addicts, and don't drink and use between meetings. Sounds easy enough, so the main reason people fail is because they do not follow directions. Some have a pre-determined mind set so strong that they actually make up their own program. Pure insanity.

John E. #3's story from Chapter Three fits well here also. How a person could come up with a chocolate bar and a six pack of beer experiment is puzzling, but not unique. What was missing from this man's life was a real recovery program. He was making up gimmicks that had no substance or proof of success. When the evil spirit came back, there was a void and he relapsed. The experiment failed.

I have heard similar thoughts from others with self produced solutions like, keep busy, clean the house, and even one guy who said told me he would just "go to his happy place." Another guy assured me that everything was fine because he buried his booze out in the woods behind his house. Forgetting the past would have been better for him, since after sobering up he remembered where he buried it and went back to get it. Recovery is actually a much simpler process, and it is already defined.

Just a note about the effectiveness of recovery programs. Information available through the internet suggest that peer support programs are ineffective, claiming Alcoholics Anonymous as an example with a 90% failure rate. Multiple studies claim only 5% to 10% of people in A.A. succeed in staying sober. Others show between 30% and 40% success rate. Sometimes it's hard to tell what the real story is, given that most of these studies have two common threads. 1) An agenda driving the study, and 2) an end result of claiming more studies need to be done. Since the purpose of most studies is to generate funding justification for more studies, personal experience is far more relevant than studies. Besides, how do you accurately study an anonymous program anyway?

An article published November 20, 2014 on WebMD was titled "Many People Who Drink a Lot Aren't Alcoholics," using a study done by the U.S. Center for Disease Control (CDC-Preventing Chronic Disease.) The study gives numbers and statistics related to drinking alcohol, and the cost impact to our culture. The article translates this information into recommended solutions; raise the price, limit the availability, education, and early detection of the problem. The study states that "doctors should be encouraged to screen their patients for excessive drinking and advise them to drink less." Brilliant, as if none of these have ever been tried before.

The study analyzed 138,100 U.S. adults between 2009 and 2011 to conclude that more studies need to be done to improve prevention. Studies can be beneficial, but they can also have ulterior motives. The point is that not all studies are objective or useful. Peer support programs have a high level of success that can only be gauged by participants, whether faith based, 12 Step, or a combination of both. And the only accurate record is in God's hands, right where it needs to be.

The statistics really point to a bigger issue though; suffering people struggle to get free. From a Christian perspective, evil spirits are having too high of a success rate. As Christians, we need to break free of studies and be about the business of fighting the spiritual battle. God will use us to help people if we are seeking and have the desire to be used. Studies will never pick up the success rate of storing treasures in heaven. We need to store up treasures daily. So read studies if you must, but get busy, because the forces of evil already are.

For those who are delivered in a moment, relapse provides a particular challenge. Most of the support for instant deliverance is connected to salvation, of receiving Christ as Savior. So if a person who has Christ in their heart relapses, what does it mean? For many, it means they run and hide. This is what we need to address as Christians instead of trying to figure out if the person was "saved" in the first place. The effectiveness of Christians dealing with addiction would increase if Schools 1 and 3 would recognize pupils that belong in the other school and make referrals to the other program.

If a person who was delivered in a moment relapses, consideration should be given to the possibility that they need more, they could be addicts who need a recovery program at School 3. Likewise, if a person attending School 3 cannot stay clean and sober, they should consider School 1. Maybe they are not an addict, and deliverance will come another way. Success in being delivered is more important than our interpretation of how it's going to happen. Playing God into the lives of others is dangerous. We are agents of God's will, not the originators.

Joe E. #7 was a fairly young man who completed a year at School 1, only to relapse within one week of returning home. Some would consider this proof that School 1 doesn't work, others might try to figure out who was to blame, both would be wrong. One Sunday morning, after the service at church, Joe E. #7 was introduced to me and one other person. As he was telling his story and getting real wound up quoting scriptures, I looked behind him at his mother who looked scared to death. Seems she had heard all this before. Within a short period of time he was asked to stop preaching and listen. The idea was proposed that he might need more than what School 1 had to offer. After some discussion we exchanged contact information and agreed to talk. Not long after we were informed that School 1 brought him back as a counselor for other pupils. It seemed to me that the void found by the evil spirit was never addressed. A referral to School 3 was probably in his best interest.

Another scripture is found in Exodus Chapter 14, which is part of the account of God's deliverance of His people from Egypt. Before this chapter, Moses has gone to Pharaoh seeking the release of the Israelites from bondage. God always hears the cries of his children; He just acts in His timing and His own way. It would have been possible for God to deliver them in a moment, but instead He demonstrated his power by delivering them through a process, 10 plagues to be exact. It seems God wanted them to see that even the most powerful influence in the world could not stand against Him. It also seems God wanted them to remember the process of their deliverance.

So the Israelites are delivered from bondage and set free. They travel to the edge of the Red Sea and camp there. The Bible tells us that God hardened Pharaoh's heart and he decided to gather his army and pursue them. The real lesson here is what the people say to Moses when they see the chariot's coming. In verses 10 through 12, the Israelites lash out at Moses and claim they should have stayed in Egypt.

"What have you done to us by bringing us out of Egypt? Didn't we say to you in Egypt, leave us alone; let us serve the Egyptians? It would be better for us to serve the Egyptians than to die in the desert." Exodus 14:12.

What? Just a short time before, they were crying out to God for deliverance. In fact, the Israelites had been slaves to Egypt for so long that not one of them actually knew what freedom was. Now they are free and want to go back because difficulty comes. How quickly they forgot their past. Not to mention how they witnessed the power of God through the 10 plagues to overthrow Pharaoh, the same guy who is now coming after them. Israel's complete lack of faith is unbelievable, but wanting to go back? While it seems really confusing, it makes perfect sense to addicts.

When people with addictions forget their past, their thinking become as delusional as the Israelites. The mind of an addict who has been delivered, whose house is swept clean and void of recovery, will think the unthinkable. When the challenges of life come, the addict will succumb to the idea that bondage to addiction wasn't so bad after all, and will return. They will forget the suffering, the loss of freedom, and the pain, just as Israel so quickly forgot what it was like in Egypt. The value of God's blessings will be blocked out by the desire for something cheap, booze or dope. Addiction will control the mind of an addict who tries to forget their past. Addicts must remember their past.

The good news in Exodus concerns how God kept his people free. The evil spirit (Pharaoh) came back with force, but God protected them. Relapse for an addict does not just happen, the process is documented in the Old and New Testaments. There is a sequence of events that takes place where a person is given opportunity to remember their past. During this time an addict can take action and stay clean and sober. Otherwise, they can continue on and suffer for it. God will not force people to choose Him, but He will provide an escape. *"A prudent man sees danger and takes refuge, but the simple keep going and suffer for it."* Proverbs 22:3, 27:12.

The rest of the story is well told. God parts the Red Sea and Israel walks through, an act of faith. The Egyptians decide to pursue them a second time, just like the evil spirit in Luke 11, but the condition here is not worse at the end. God's people pass through the sea, Pharaoh's army does not. Forgetting their past almost cost them their lives. It's the same for addicts.

Another recovery scripture in Corinthians builds on the concept of an escape. It is a commonly quoted scripture that holds insights to why the past is so important to remember: *"No temptation has seized you except what is common to man. And God is faithful; he will not let you be tempted beyond what you can bear. But when you are tempted, he will also provide a way out so that you can stand up under it."* I Corinthians 10:13.

A quick study of this verse in most any concordance will explain the application. The picture here is of a fire escape, which is best understood by reading the previous verse: *"So, if you think you are standing firm, be careful that you don't fall."* I Corinthians 10:12.

The outcome of temptation is like being caught in a burning building. Truly God's incredible grace is the main theme here. He cannot tempt anyone, so if we get into trouble because we follow temptation into a bad situation, it's our own fault. Yet, He will still provide a way out. So why do addicts relapse if God has provided an escape? Because after they get delivered, they run back into the burning building. Forgetting the past means forgetting there was a fire, and that the temptation led to trouble. While this seems impossible, it is not. Israel forgot what it was like in Egypt. Addicts forget what it was like before deliverance. This scripture and principle can apply whether a person is delivered in a moment or through a process. Forgetting leads to relapse and people get burned.

"However, if we intentionally put ourselves in the way of temptation, then we put God to the test – and this is sin." Dr. Grant C Richison.

Jane E. #6 was a woman in a recovery program, an alcoholic. In a discussion with other alcoholics one day, she described how she went to a bar but later realized she had made a bad decision. She told of how she prayed to God to get her out of there, and God delivered. Sounds good, except another alcoholic put her in her place. Seems that Jane E. #6 had been observed going to the bar more than once, and was told by a more experienced alcoholic in recovery that she was playing with fire. She didn't listen and eventually relapsed. This is a good example of why the way of escape disappears, by continuing to run back into the temptation.

Another example is Jewel E. #1, an addict. She decided that it was a good idea to go to the club where she used to drink and use, for the purpose of telling the drunks about Jesus. She spent a lot of time in the club trying to reach the lost for Christ. The outcome was inevitable, she drank. Prior to the relapse, I told her that her evangelism of the club was not a good idea, especially since she had just a short time sober. But she decided to forget the advice and her past, and ran back into the same type of temptation. The final condition was worse than the first.

A solution is only as good as it holds up under the worst of circumstances. This is where people need to land who think they have one answer for everyone. Finding a way to help people with addictions should not lead to prideful thinking, which in turn leads to arrogance. Christians need to remember that God's will is to deliver people from addictions. How they will be delivered is up to Him. Some of the solutions being provided do not hold up in the worst of circumstances.

While conversing with Joe E. #2, who was delivered instantly from alcohol and drugs, I shared about how God had delivered me through a process. Unable to accept this truth, Joe E. #2 proclaimed with a loud voice and wavering arms "You're Free." I agreed, but as the discussion continued it became obvious that he was stuck on a different solution, and because God's name was on it there could be no other. Could you imagine this young expert telling a female addict like Jane E. #5, who was prostituted by her mother for drugs, that the solution to her problems was "You're Free." Remember, Jane E. #5 is an associate pastor's wife who found freedom by remembering her past. She didn't have to go back to Egypt to find freedom, she just had to do more than sweep the house clean. Now she is able to be honest with others about her skeletons, then put them away until they're needed again. Joe E. #2 needed to realize that his solution would not hold up under the worst of circumstances. And while in real life he is a graduate of a Bible college, he's still a freshman in the School of Addiction with a whole lot to learn.

Another recovery scripture in Romans deals with the mind. Recalling the past is obviously a function of the memory. Even though it affects us emotionally, spiritually, and physically, it always starts in the mind. The brain is complex, and with all we've learned through science and medical research, there are still some who throw out the baby with the bathwater when it comes to psychology. Words of the Bible support and confirm what modern science has more recently identified. Christians are not alone in this rejection. Dr. Earl Henslin, a respected authority on addictions and brain chemistry, said "Psychologist are the only part of the medical profession that will treat an organ without looking at it." At that time, he was referring to the rejection of SPECT imaging for treating disorders.

In Romans Chapter 8, the apostle Paul wrote about two sides of the mind, carnal and spiritual. Which one is going to win? Only one can, only one will. This is where the battle of addiction is fought; an addict must remember this because the road to relapse is opened by a condition called the" mental obsession." This condition explains why someone can block out God's blessings because of an obsession with the high. Science has accurately identified two sides of the brain, each with their own function. SPECT imaging is a 3D color picture of the brain's activity, which confirmed that the compulsive (carnal) nature resides in one part of the brain, and our connection to God (spiritual) resides in the other. Exactly what Paul wrote about 2,000 years ago: *"Those who live according to the sinful nature have their minds set on what the nature desires; but those who live in accordance with the Spirit have their mind set on what the Spirit desires. The mind of sinful man is death, but the mind controlled by the Spirit is life and peace; the sinful mind is hostile to God. It does not submit to God's law, nor can it do so."* Romans 8:5-7.

It has also been established that our natural human instincts reside in one side of the brain. This is why addiction will cause a person to ignore the basic instincts for survival and relationships. Want to know why an addict will pursue the high in spite of risking their life or losing personal relationships? It is because addiction blocks out these natural instincts. Even though it's a delusion, and a cheap one compared to the value of life and family, addiction wins out. Addicts will act as if they do not care, which is not the case. It's just that God given instincts are being altered by the introduction of toxic chemicals. What the family and friends see is a chemically altered version of their loved one, the chemicals are causing a malfunction in the mind. The carnal mind is in control, it is at war with God and will not submit to His laws. This is why solid treatment programs are critical in addiction for detoxing a person off the chemicals, so the spiritual mind can establish control.

It is really not too hard to understand how this works. Examples have been developed for decades. Movies with someone having a devil on one shoulder and an angel on the other. Which one will win? Only one can. Each is like a lawyer stating their case and trying to persuade the outcome. An addict who is clean and sober without a recovery program only has the little red guy to listen to, and before long several more with the same agenda.

Another example is "red dog, blue dog," using the analogy of both being inside of a person. Whichever one we feed will be in control. One is good, the other is bad. Which one will win? Only one can, only one will. It is told that the one we feed is the one that gains strength and wins. While this is more widely used to gain a daily focus on life, it is an example of the idea that two different forces are at work within us, and that one or the other is going to gain control. A spiritual mind leads to life; the carnal mind leads to death. An addict must understand this and take action, or at least be willing to follow directions until they understand.

Why is it that people with a common struggle getting together and sharing their testimony helps overcome addiction? Because it reduces the obsession in the carnal mind and increases the solution in the spiritual mind. Support group dynamics are amazing. They obviously work, but how? One part of the answer relates to how people share at meetings. One person talks, everyone else listens. This does not guarantee people won't get off focus or become banner wavers, but at all times it turns off the carnal mind and turns on the spiritual mind.

The best example I ever witnessed of this dynamic took place in our teen recovery support group. It is a tough age to work with, and our recovery program was blessed with a young woman who led the group each week. On one occasion she was away and I had to lead the group. I went, greeted everyone, and sat down without giving any directions. For about 10 minutes the teens talked about all kinds of stuff, boyfriend, girlfriend, money, etc. I then asked if this was how the group was run each week; one said no and produced the book they used. The book had a support group guideline, so I suggested we use the guide.

What happened next was surprising, amazing, and confirms how support groups shift people's thoughts from one side of the brain to the other. When the "rules" for sharing were followed, there was no more talk of previous topics. Each one of the teenagers in the group took time to share about personal issues, challenges, and even how some things were getting better. A completely different discussion with a simple change. That's what support groups do, bring out the inner person by activating the spiritual mind.

Another application of Romans 8:5-7 in addiction recovery is that remembering the past can prevent false confidence. It is never a good idea for an addict to say "I will never use or drink again." It might sound like confidence, but it's dangerous. If an addict forgets the "thorn in the flesh" then they also forget what happens when the thorn is triggered. Part of remembering the past ties directly to the war that is going on in our minds, and goes back to II Peter 2:20 from Chapter One, "*as a dog returns to its vomit, so a fool returns to his folly.*" It is better for an addict to take the road of gratitude than confidence. Besides, if sobriety comes through God's grace, what do we have to be confident about? Learning to be humble is another requirement of recovery. Confidence in the outcome of the future is based on false pride. Never say never when it comes to addiction.

While attending a recovery conference, I heard a speaker say that "most of us don't realize how far off the mark we really are." He was referring to the mental block that addiction creates in the mind. Christian addicts struggle with this tremendously, trying to reconcile why faith in Christ does not produce sobriety.

So many opinions floating around with just as many ideas about the solution. But this speaker hit the nail on the head.

The main reason I think Christians struggle with addictions is because they think they are pretty good people that just need a little cleaning up, when the truth is, they need a major overhaul. So far off the mark of where God wants them to be, but unable to be honest about it. This is denial, which is a function of the mind, the carnal mind.

There is one thing I have learned about this principle in my own life. The closer I get to the mark, the farther away it is. Clarity in the spiritual mind has revealed this. For Christians the mark is Christ, and someone with an active addiction isn't as close as they think they are. With recovery comes clarity, a true sense that the mark is farther away even though the process is bringing us closer by the day. The mark does not move, just our perspective changes from denial to truth. If a Christian with an active addiction can be honest about where they are in God's will, then their chances of achieving recovery increases. "*...like a true spiritual racer, not minding what he had received by grace...but straining forward, as it were, with all his force and skill, casting himself like a dart towards the mark.*" Commentary by Matthew Poole.

The story about Joe E. #4 from Chapter Two applies here also. The Christian who was addicted to cocaine but wanted to conduct an interview to determine if I was good enough to help him. It seems he was not ready to be honest about how far off the mark he really was. "*The truth will set you free*" *(John 8:24)*, but it might upset your denial. I have talked with many Christians like him.

Working to help people with addictions is tough and demanding, the success stories are incredible, and the failures are heartbreaking. Some people just do not want to know the truth even though they say otherwise, including Christians who are being controlled by the carnal mind. They "*have their minds set on what the nature desires*" (Romans 8:5). They are trying to solve the problem with the problem. Using the carnal mind to solve a problem being produced by the carnal mind does not work. When addicts are active in their addiction, they need to use their spiritual mind to stop thinking they know the answer, start listening, and following directions.

A mom from our church called and asked if I would talk with her son. He was struggling with drugs and alcohol. She told me he wanted to talk with both of us, so I went to their home. It was an ambush. He did not know I was coming. I could have left but felt led by God to stay. After about 15 minutes of listening to their bickering and fielding his cheap insults aimed at me, I asked mom if I could talk with him alone. She agreed and went to another part of the house. I told this young man my testimony, what is was like for me before recovery, what happened, and what it is like now. In other words, I used my past. I took the skeletons out of the closet and showed them to him. Addicts can do that as there is no need to hide from the past. I then asked him if he wanted to go to a recovery meeting that was starting in 20 minutes. He agreed, so we let mom know we were leaving.

You would think she would be happy, but she was not. In fact, she protested, "I've been trying to get him to go to a meeting for two years and you did it in a half an hour. That's not fair." What could I say. I let her down easy. "You're not an addict," was my response. In that situation, my past was my greatest asset. It connected me to a feisty young man who minutes before was only interested in taking verbal jabs.

Addicts must remember their past, not only because it is a powerful tool for helping others, but it also prevents going back to Egypt.

CHAPTER FIVE

12 Step Recovery is not a Path to Heaven or Hell

My testimony:

I grew up in northern California in the 1960's and 70's, in the middle of what I would later come to know as a "drug culture." For me, it was just normal. There were lots of fun stories and crazy episodes. Most of my junior high and high school years were spent partying with friends. It would be easy to label who I was as a problem youth, except that during junior high while I was learning about drugs and alcohol first hand, I was also an honor roll student, block letter athlete, and captain of some of the sports teams I played sports on. Prior to those years from ages five to thirteen, I was active in competitive swimming (AAU) and other sports in elementary school. There were plenty of other youths like myself where I grew up.

By the time I reached high school, I had found white powder and pills. Cocaine and crank (methamphetamine) were the ticket to fun. By 11th grade, I was no longer interested in school and sports, but did maintain employment partly because I had learned a good work ethic at home and partly because I needed money to party.

Home was by all appearances a good place. We had a nice house, good clothes, and never went hungry. My parents took us lots of places and participated in our sports and school events. There was really no reason or tragic circumstances to blame for heading in the direction of addiction, other than I was enjoying myself and ignoring what had happened to some other people. I never really went the path of a criminal, being locked up didn't appeal to me. I just wanted to have fun and pursue the next crazy idea to have a good time.

At my high school graduation ceremony as the last person was getting their diploma, I dropped a military grade red smoke bomb in the graduate seats on the field. Since my last name starts with "H", I was strategically located in the middle. When the smoke cleared there was nothing but knocked over chairs, a circle of students around them, and teachers in disbelief. There were no camcorders or smart phones back then, and only a few close friends knew. I got away with it.

After graduation there were no plans for the future, so I joined the Navy a month later, arriving in boot camp five days after that. Compulsive actions did not seem out of the ordinary. Once my mind was made up, it was full steam ahead. After four years of service on submarines and receiving accommodations and meritorious advancements, I was caught on a urinalysis for using cocaine. Since junior high my life had been a contradiction of extremes, except now the consequences were getting serious.

I lost my "Dolphins" (submarine qualification), lost stripes, time, and money. A few years earlier I had broken the record for qualification on the oldest sub in the fleet at the time (USS Gudgeon, SS 567) by qualifying 17 weeks ahead of schedule. There was the celebration at the Sub Vets of World War II convention in Sacramento, CA. Our boat had navigated the Sacramento River to attend the event, my parents and family watched as my Dolphins were put on by a Retired Rear Admiral from WWII. Very promising military future for a young man of 20, which evaporated in the pursuit of getting drunk and high.

With my good record and history in the service, I was given a chance to finish my enlistment and get out with an honorable discharge if I could "keep my nose clean" for six months. So I did. In the year after getting out of the service, I was married and had my first son. It was also a time I committed to staying away from booze and drugs to have a better life. All went well for a year, then a little drinking, then a little drugs, and within a few months, disaster. The train wreck came fast. I would later understand the progressive nature of addiction. I lost a good job, and no longer cared. All I wanted was to get drunk and high. I was going to figure out how to have a family, a job, and plenty of drugs. That's all I wanted. It took about six months to get to the lowest place in life I have ever been.

I was living back at my parent's house away from my family, which was now two sons. The mental insanity was more than I could take. I wanted to stop, but kept using instead. So I decided one evening that ending my life was the way out. Late at night, I was walking back to my parent's house and was ready to step in front of a semi truck coming down the road. I actually stepped to make the plunge, and a thought entered my mind: "I'm wearing my friend's jacket that he won as the MVP in a large baseball tournament. If I do this, I'm going to mess up his jacket." All that in a split second, I hesitated and the truck went by.

The next morning, I cried out to God in a state of desperation. The room I was in was suddenly filled with an overwhelming presence of peace. The hole in the middle of my gut was not there. Everything changed that day. I realized who put that thought in my head the night before, it was not by chance. Other recent events started making sense. God was working with me before I realized it. That was March 1, 1987. A few days later, through the guidance of a local pastor, I went to my first recovery meeting. At 25 years of age, my life started over.

The life I had with God through church and a recovery program was incredible. I had a spiritual connection with my Heavenly Father that changed everything, and I could daily live with His guidance and help, which I desperately needed. I was also pretty rough on the edges, had serious issues with anger and could not get along with other people. But I was working at changing. Both church and recovery were key to that change. Some people experience these changes instantly, mine came over time through a combination of works and faith.

Within a few days of getting clean and sober, I was hired at a manufacturing plant into the maintenance department. It was just the environment God wanted me in, a daily opportunity to grow. After a while, some other guys were getting hired into maintenance at the plant who were Christians. Soon after, the Playboy magazines on the break table were replaced by Bibles, and the centerfolds were no longer visible on the outside of the lockers. Seems that conscience was at work. The influence of more experienced Christians was good for my growth, and a few began to ask questions about my being "saved." I really wasn't quite sure what that meant; after all I did have a relationship with God so I resisted their inquiries. During that time, I asked my pastor what it meant to be saved, and he assured me that I probably was. But God had other plans.

One weekend I was invited to a prayer meeting at a small church by one of the guys I worked with. I had been to this church before so it was nothing unusual. Just before leaving the house I got a call from another friend, the late Ralph Eichenbaum. He was a minister, a brother in recovery, and a mentor for me personally. His conversation that day seemed out of the ordinary and he said, "God bless you tonight, Steve." He knew where I was going and somehow had an intuition as it turned out that he had been praying for something specific to happen in my life.

When I arrived at the prayer service, I saw familiar and unfamiliar faces. I had met the pastor before and was glad to see him. The church was a small one up in the mountains outside where I lived in a lake community. At the beginning of the service, the pastor gave his testimony about going to church for two years and thinking that all was good because he was experiencing God in his life. But someone told him the Gospel, the truth about Jesus Christ and why He died on the cross, and more importantly why His resurrection was the path to eternal life. God had my attention from the moment the pastor started speaking. It was unmistakable that He wanted something from me. When the pastor explained the Gospel, I knew what God wanted, to accept His son Jesus as my Savior. He wanted me to know that my path so far had led me to the cross, but I had to make a decision to accept what He was offering.

The pastor's testimony was not long; it didn't need to be. When he asked if anyone wanted to receive Christ to come forward and pray with him, I went. It was emotionally overwhelming and he could tell. I just cried and kept saying, "I didn't know." What I can now appreciate about my friends is that they were praying for me while I was rejecting their inquiries about salvation. So many things changed after that day. Reading the Bible was different, so was praying and serving God. But it was also confusing. How could I have been clean and sober for a year and a half with the clear presence of God in my life without being saved? It would take some time to understand it all. Especially since the Bible says no man comes to the Father except through the Son.

In the simplest terms I had a relationship with my Heavenly Father, who wanted me to meet His Son, so that I could have the presence of the Holy Spirit in my life, and spend eternity with Him in heaven. Scripture makes this possible to understand; we don't have to make it up or try to figure it all out.

If you seek the Father, you will find the Son.

That was over 25 years ago and the importance of that day is still being played out. After many years at the plant, I went into the ministry full time. I meet Christians all the time who cannot understand why their faith in Christ will not keep them clean and sober. Likewise, I meet people in recovery programs who think their sobriety and spiritual connection to God is all they need for eternity. I also meet debaters and modern day Pharisees, who thinks it's their job to redefine my testimony. Fortunately, I learned that my relationship with God is more important than other people's opinions, so their objections only strengthen my faith. Besides, my ministry and calling is for the suffering person who is asking for help and does not have all the answers, the ones who are desperate. It is part of the character of my Savior, to seek the lost and the sick. It clearly was not in my life without Him.

The Gospel is a subject that has everything to do with our identity as children of God. As such, Satan has targeted this subject to cause large scale confusion. One thing we can count on, if God is for it then Satan is against it, no matter what the subject. If that subject leads to eternity with God, then the opposition will be strong. Personal identity is certainly under attack in the world on multiple levels, with gender identity leading the way. We need a clear understanding of who we are in our Heavenly Father's eyes. Eternity depends on it.

What is our true identity? First, we are created in the image of God which applies to all mankind. "*So God created mankind in his own image, in the image of God he created them; male and female, he created them.*" *Genesis 1:27.*

Being created in God's image means that when we are born on this earth, it is the beginning of our individual life. Until we were conceived there was no "me" or "you." But after conception, an individual is formed that has a unique identity. There has never and will never be another you. Even if multiple children are born to the same parents, they each have a unique identity. All mankind has one thing in common, we are all created in the image of God. For some, this is all they want, but in God's eyes it is only the beginning.

Jesus explained the next step to Nicodemus in John Chapter 3. He told the seeking Pharisee that he "must be born again." Confused by the idea, Jesus had to explain further

"Flesh gives birth to flesh, but the spirit gives birth to spirit. You should not be surprised at my saying, 'You must be born again.'" John 3:6-7.

- To be born of the flesh is to be born in the image of God.
- To be born of the Spirit is to make a decision to accept Jesus Christ as Savior.
- Then the Holy Spirit comes and lives within us, and we become children of God.

It is in the process of this simple plan that Satan inserts his agenda: lying. The idea of being born into the world making you a child of God is popular, but false. If this were true, there would be no need for Christ or the Holy Spirit, and the only one who doesn't need them is called the father of lies, and that is Satan himself. *"When he lies, he speaks his native language, for he is a liar and the father of lies."* John 8:44.

The word Gospel points to truth. By definition, it is *"something accepted or promoted as infallible truth,"* Webster's Dictionary. Accepting or rejecting the truth is a matter of personal choice, but that does not change the content of the truth. The only way you can do that is to lie. God's truth about His son Jesus Christ is the Gospel, an infallible truth that originated in heaven given to us as humans to make a choice. Being a child of God depends on the choice you make, not the choice your parents made that brought you into this world.

"And you also were included in Christ when you heard the message of truth, the gospel of your salvation. When you believed, you were marked in him with a seal, the promised Holy Spirit." Ephesians 1:13.

"   *Now it is God who makes both us and you stand firm in Christ. He anointed us, set his seal of ownership on us, and put his spirit into our hearts as a deposit, guaranteeing what is to come.*" II Corinthians 1:21-22.

"*The Spirit himself testifies with our spirit that we are God's children.*" Romans 8:16.

"*Yet to all who received him, to those who believed in his name, he gave the right to become children of God--children born not of natural descent, nor of human decision or a husband's will, but born of God.*" John 1:12-13.

"*For it is by grace are you have been saved, through faith, and this is not from yourselves, it is the gift of God--not by works, so that no one can boast.*" Ephesians 2:8-9.

- God created all of mankind in His image, described in the Bible as born of a human decision (born of the flesh).
- We are all given a choice to accept the Gospel, the truth about Christ as our Savior. It is our decision to accept or reject it.
- When we accept the Gospel we are born spiritually (born again). The Holy Spirit then lives in our hearts as God's seal of ownership, and we become children of God, members of His family for all eternity.

Jesus Christ is a simple solution to a complicated problem. Acceptance of the solution is our problem. Of course, many ideas exist in the world about how all this plays out, and there is plenty of debate to cause confusion. What needs to be considered are the words of Philippians Chapter Two, which are frequently misquoted by leaving out the middle: "*That at the name of Jesus every knee shall bow, <u>in heaven and on earth and under the earth</u>, and every tongue confess that Jesus Christ is Lord.*" Philippians 2:10-11.

Most of the time, Christians quote this scripture as "every knee will bow and every tongue confess" without stating the underlined section above. But taking away from God's Word means removing part of the truth. Every knee will bow to Jesus, not just the ones on earth, but also the ones in heaven and hell. Nothing in all creation gets around this truth.

There are many ways to present the Gospel to someone as long as it holds true to the message. In my mom's final days on earth, she requested that the "Good News" be told at her funeral. She knew where she was going, and wanted others to hear the "the Gospel of the Lord Jesus Christ." I knew there would be people in attendance with all kinds of ideas about how to get to heaven. After praying for wisdom and trusting God for guidance, I presented the Gospel at her service in this manner:

In heaven, there is a book called the Lamb's Book of Life. In it are written the names of the people that are going to heaven. In order to get your name in the book, you have to be perfect. We have a problem. We all have a problem. We are all sinners, and it only takes one sin to not have your name written in that book. We needed a way to get our names written in that Book. Jesus said, "I am the way, the truth, and the life; no man comes to the Father but by me." There is nothing you can do to earn your way into heaven. It is an insolvable problem, but Jesus Christ solved the problem.

When He died on the cross he paid the penalty for our sins, and three days later when He rose from the grave He gained the victory over death to give us eternal life. That is the Gospel, it is the truth. You can accept it or reject it, it's up to you. But to enter heaven you not only have to trust in something outside of yourself, which is Christ Himself, but you also have to invite Him in. Because every knee is going to bow, "in heaven, and on earth, and under the earth." You can do it now or do it later, but later is too late. The decision to accept the Gospel has to be made before you die.

John 3:16 states "God so loved the world that he gave his one and only Son, that whoever believes in him shall not perish but have everlasting life." The "world" is you, because the only part of creation that God wants to save is the souls of human beings. Everything else will pass away.*

If you want to make a decision the terms are simple, just believe and ask. The words can vary as long as the message isn't changed. One example would be:

"Lord Jesus, I am a sinner and I cannot change myself. I believe that you died for my sins, and that you rose from the dead to give me eternal life. I ask you to forgive me and come into my heart as my Savior. I trust that my name will be written in your Book of Life. Thank you for loving me. Amen".

If you made the decision and accepted God's plan of salvation, then there is a lot of rejoicing taking place right now. Share your decision with someone else that can not only rejoice with you, but also be a support and encouragement to you as a child of God.

Jesus himself said *"I tell you, there is rejoicing in the presence of the angels of God over one sinner who repents."* Luke 15:10.

The subject that becomes necessary to address then is the belief that all people who have the presence of God in their life are going to heaven. Wouldn't that be nice, but it is not true. It also forces some clarification on the scripture where Jesus says "no one come to the Father except by me." Does this mean that God the Father is never involved in the lives of people until after they accept Jesus Christ as their Savior? Some believe so, but it doesn't hold up under scrutiny. In fact, it fails miserably in light of the many other scriptures.

If Jesus ascended back to heaven (John 20:17), then "coming to the Father" is our entrance into heaven after death. But to suggest that until the Gospel is accepted through Christ that no one can communicate with their Heavenly Father, or until that point He is not involved in any individual's life, is absurd. A prime example of contempt prior to investigation.

The Creator is not absent from His creation, He is always at work, especially where souls are concerned. This is specifically where Christians close the door on reaching people in recovery programs with the Gospel, by telling them that the God they know is not God at all. That He is just some "nebulous" being with no definition. But this doesn't hold up under close scrutiny either. Pure contempt.

Also, people in recovery programs need to understand that because they have a testimony of God working in their life does not mean that they have eternal life. *"That which is born of the flesh is flesh and of the spirit is spirit, you must be born again."* Nicodemus knew God but not Jesus, so the response of Christians towards those in secular recovery should be the same as Christ to Nicodemus. Jesus didn't tell him that he didn't know God, he told him there was more to God than he knew.

Jesus explained this in the book of John Chapter 5. He describes both the distinct working of the Father and the connection to His Son.

"So, because Jesus was doing these things on the Sabbath, the Jewish leaders began to persecute him. In his defense Jesus said to them, 'My Father is always at his work to this very day, and I too am working.

"Very truly I tell you, the Son can do nothing by himself; he can do only what he sees his Father doing, because whatever the Father does the Son also does. For the Father loves the Son and shows him all he does.'" John 5:16-17,19-20.

Since the misuse of truth is at the core of misunderstanding in addictions, there needs to be some investigation done to present the truth. Most if not all the confusion is because of someone taking a basic truth to dysfunctional extreme. False statements or doctrines are not the issue.

For Christians a good question is, "Does anyone use the same Bible you do, but in a way you don't agree with?" If the answer is yes, then quit reading the Bible and stop going to church. After all, someone is misusing the truth. The reasoning here doesn't hold up very well. No one would quit using the Bible as a resource just because someone else is using it in a different way. It's the same with books and literature for recovery programs. Just because someone is misusing a book doesn't make the book wrong, it makes the person wrong. So why do so many Christians take opposition with recovery programs? Because they only know of the misuses and not the actual content. Some people in secular recovery have taken the core principles of these life changing programs to dysfunctional extremes, so the conclusion of some Christians is the whole program is bad. Neither one is right.

Twice a year there is an event held in the mountains for people in recovery. It has some limitations. It's for a particular recovery program for men, and only has space for 280 people. There is always a waiting list. I was invited by a good friend to go attend the event with several men from our area. It was amazing to see so many people seeking God and living in the grace of being clean and sober. One morning there was a "sunrise service" for those who wanted to attend. It was held in an open amphitheater that was a short hike from the camp. A very peaceful, quiet, beautiful setting, and well attended.

There were some men gathered up front with a guitar to lead in some traditional hymns, and a man who to lead the service. Before he started there were a couple simple requests, one was that if anyone attending believed that their higher power was a door knob or coffee cup to please keep it to themselves. Anyone the least bit familiar with the stereotypes of secular recovery programs understands why he said this. Some people have interpreted the books in secular recovery to arrive at a conclusion; they can create their own god. This is pure contempt for the principles of recovery and absolute misuse of the books, but somehow best known by those outside the programs.

Just like it takes some simple review of the Word of God to find truth, it also takes some basic review of the writings where recovery started to find the source of these errors. Doing so will help clarify that the core principles are actually solid when compared with the Bible.

In the story of Bill Wilson, co-founder of Alcoholic Anonymous, he describes how a member of the Oxford Group influenced his life. These were Christian groups helping people with alcohol problems, and the man who visited Bill one day was a friend who he previously drank with, but was now sober through the Oxford Group program. Bill was still drinking despite efforts to quit. During the conversation, Bill was presented with the idea of choosing his own understanding of God as a starting point, instead of trying to embrace someone else's understanding. Somehow, that got through to Bill where other attempts had failed. Not long after, Bill had an experience in the hospital where he surrendered his life to God.

The key here is to understand that Bill never thought, implied, or desired to "create his own god." In the original text of the A.A. program, known as the Big Book, Bill's own statements in his story confirm this:

"It was only a matter of being willing to believe in a Power greater than myself. Nothing more was required to make a beginning. I saw that growth could start from that point."

First, notice the word "Power" is capitalized. Every time that God is referenced in the writing of the Big Book, His name is capitalized. This is important in clarifying how this book has been misused by people to create their own god. Other examples of capitalized names include Creator, Heavenly Father, Father of Light, Maker, etc.

The Big Book describes God as having all knowledge (omniscient) and all power (omnipotent), being present everywhere (omnipresent), yet having concern with each of us individually. It tells us that God can do things for people that they cannot do for themselves. Dependence upon God over all other things in life is required; over money, family and career. The consistency in the character of the God of the Bible and the God of the Big Book is striking. Some of the writings emphasized that the power needed to recover could not have originated inside of us; it must have come from something greater. It also states *"But there is One who has all power--that One is God. May you find Him now."*

The Gospel of Christ is not covered in the Alcoholic Anonymous' Big Book, to which all Christians should applaud. If it was, then secular recovery programs would be a path to heaven. Instead, there are references in this book pointing people to the Gospel but not providing it. There is a great opportunity missed when Christians criticize secular recovery for not having the Gospel. It is not supposed to; it never was. It is also not a path to hell either since it offers no solution that is eternal.

Soon after the writing of the Big Book people started misusing the truth and creating confusion. The same problem was occurring before the apostle Paul finished his life. In the first days of the church that Christ came to establish, people immediately started misusing the truth for their own means. Did this change the truth? Of course not. But it did require some additional writings to re-establish the truth. Such was the case with the Big Book, and co-founder Bill Wilson wrote the "12 Steps and 12 Traditions," also known as the "12 and 12."

In this second book from the A.A. program, the misuse of truth is addressed. Some people decided that the group itself could be their higher power. Since a group is stronger than an individual, this seemed to fit nicely for people who wanted to avoid the God subject or take the idea to a dysfunctional extreme. Paul had to address a few issues too. Christians who thought they could achieve perfection, and others who wanted to keep the old ways and combine them with the new. In other words, change the truth to fit their own way of thinking.

The 12 and 12 was developed with several ideas in mind, one of which was to clarify truth. On page 109, Bill Wilson wrote, *"we could predict that the doubter who still claimed that he hadn't got the 'spiritual angle,' and who still considered his well-loved A.A. group the higher power, would presently love God and call Him by name."*

The intention to re-focus on God as the higher power is clearly stated in the fact that Bill did not capitalize those two words on this page of the 12 and 12, and identifies anyone who thinks the group is their god as a doubter. Not only that, but he is trying to redirect the person to call God by name. Misuse of truth does not change the truth. It makes the person who is trying to change the truth wrong.

John E. #9 is a member of a secular recovery program. While attending the same retreat in the mountains that I attended, John E. #9 decided to visit the local town one evening with a group of people. The local population is small, so it seems they know when this particular event is taking place. While in town John E. #9 went into an activity being hosted by a local church. His appearance gave him away to the Christians, and he was told they didn't want "his type" at their gathering and asked him to leave. Comments by the locals confirmed they didn't want anyone around who believed God was a door knob or a coffee cup. Contempt in this case is too kind; brood of vipers is more accurate. Instead of seeing an opportunity to embrace a human being who knew God and trying to introduce him to Jesus, they just wanted to crucify him. A visible expression of the love of Christ would have been a better choice. Besides, they never knew if he was a Christian or not, the verdict was out before the trial started. They were acting more like Pharisees than Christians.

In the discussion that takes place in John Chapter 3 about being born again, Nicodemus asks Jesus "how can this be?" Jesus responds by throwing down some hard truth for this religious leader to accept. *"You are Israel's teacher,"* said Jesus, *"and do you not understand these things? Very truly I tell you, we speak of what we know, and we testify to what we have seen, but still you people do not accept our testimony."* John 3:10-11.

It's the same as people in recovery programs testifying to what they know and what they have seen, being rejected by Christian leaders because they do not understand and asked "how can this be?" Never doubt the love of God for suffering people. As far as testimonies, there are people in churches and recovery programs that give testimonies that do not line up with God's standards as set forth in the Bible. That makes the individual wrong, not all testimonies. When someone in recovery points to the grace of God as the source of their ability to not drink or use, rejoice.

So what about the idea that anyone with evidence of God's presence in their lives are going to heaven. Recovery programs are not the path to heaven. Simply put, there is no A.A. meetings in heaven; there is no need for any. There are no drugs or alcohol there, no overdoses, no families being destroyed. All of this is sin and will never be present in heaven. The purpose of recovery programs is to provide a way for people to live clean and sober on earth, or address one of the many issues recovery works on, all of which ends when we take our last breath. But salvation in Jesus Christ starts on earth and continues into heaven for eternity.

"Turning to a different gospel-- which is really no gospel at all. Evidently some people are throwing you into confusion and are trying to pervert the gospel of Christ. But even if we or an angel from heaven should preach to you a gospel other than the one we preached to you, let him be eternally condemned." Galatians 1:6-8.

Recovery programs as a path to heaven is a made up Gospel, which is really no Gospel at all. But is this really much different than Christians making up ways to get to heaven that contradict the Scriptures? Not really. And if we're going to avoid organizations that have some people misrepresenting the truth, then we all have to avoid places we should be in. Would someone stop going to doctors just because some doctors are bad? Or quit eating in restaurants because one served a bad meal? Why not quit paying taxes because some government officials misrepresented the truth. Where do we draw the line? Where is the consistency? *"If you hold to my teachings, you are really my disciples. Then you will know the truth, and the truth will set you free."* John 8:31.

The Truth about the Cultural Compass:

Author Don Richardson wrote a book called "Eternity in their Hearts." He takes the scripture from Ecclesiastes 3:11, where the Bible states that God has put eternity into the hearts of people, so that we will seek Him. We all have within our hearts the fundamental idea of God. As one minister put it, "I don't want to know why you don't believe in God, but I would like to know what made you not believe." We have to push the concept of God out of our conscience in order to not believe.

Richardson presents the concept of a "cultural compass," one that points to God. He uses this analogy to show how God has put various symbols, rituals, and customs in cultures throughout history that point to Him. It is a fascinating book that is well researched, giving specific examples. The basic idea is that God put these "compasses" in place as a personal "finger print," to show that He has not left any culture void of Himself. It's his seal of authenticity. If this is true, then A.A. would have specific items pointing directly to Him and not away from Him. There are in fact several.

As discussed, anytime the Big Book referenced God it did so with a capitalized name. This in itself is consistent with Scripture since false gods are never capitalized.

Next, the 12 Steps themselves have three references to God by using the words Power, God, and Him/His. These steps are the core of the program, and God is described in three persons. This is consistent with the Trinity of the Bible, Father, Son, and Holy Spirit.

Another example is in what is called the "3rd Step Prayer," which partially states *"take away my difficulties, that victory over them may bear witness to those I would help of Thy Power, Thy Love, and Thy Way of life."* Taking the same focus on the God of the Bible as the Trinity, this prayer goes a step further in describing God as Power, Love, and the Way. It does not take a theological degree to see the connection. Where else is God described as "the Way" except in the Bible where Jesus described himself as the Way. And here again we have the word Power capitalized.

The "Power greater than ourselves" statement, according to the original literature, is not pointing to some nebulous god, some door knob or coffee cup. It is not opening the door to making up your own god. It is power, the power of God himself that is required to succeed in recovery. And as if God needed Christian recovery programs to straighten out what He had right in the first place, several of the most prominent ones have taken the capital "P" out of the word power in the 2nd Step. Evidently, this helps to clarify the phrase as not meaning God, when keeping it in actually helps clarify His influence on the 12 Steps. It also represents his "fingerprint" of authenticity, consistent with the Biblical descriptions of God. The writers of the book wanted to point people towards Christ, but not replace the Gospel with another one.

These are just a few examples of the many correlations between recovery programs and the Bible. Chapter Six will cover 12 Common Bonds in detail. The main point here is that the God who authored the Bible was present in the forming of the 12 Steps, not as a replacement or equivalent to the Gospel, but as a reflection of Himself pointing people to the Gospel. And while some people have chosen to interpret these programs as a path to heaven, scores of others have not, and have found Christ. If you seek the Father you will find the Son, not the devil. Otherwise recovery would be divided against itself, and according to the truth established in God's Holy Word, it could not stand. *"Every kingdom divided against itself will be ruined, and every city or household divided against itself will not stand."* Matthew 12:25.

There are plenty of resources available which try to prove that 12 Step Recovery is a path to hell. A solid example of contempt prior to investigation. How can a program that directs people to seek God be leading them towards hell? It would be divided against itself, and according to the truth established in God's Holy Word, could not stand. 12 Step Recovery is not a path to hell, it never has been and it never will be. Jesus had the same problem. It is actually a repetitive problem, because there is nothing new under the sun. *"What has been will be again, what has been done will be done again; there is nothing new under the sun."* Ecclesiastes 1:9.

People tried to accuse Jesus of being connected to the devil. In fact, it was done by religious people who couldn't figure out how He was performing miracles. It was their default answer, blame it on the devil. When people say by their testimony that the obsession to self destruct through addiction has been removed by the power of God, then the modern day Pharisees are attributing God's divine work to Satan. Jesus pointed out that such a position is not only wrong, but actually reveals the source of the real problem. They failed to see the work of God, even when it was in plain view. *"If Satan drives out Satan, he is divided against himself. How then can his kingdom stand? And if I drive out demons by Beelzebub, by whom do your people drive them out? So then, they will be your judges. But if it is by the Spirit of God that I drive out demons, then the kingdom of God has come upon you."* Matthew 12:26-27.

Bible Commentaries on Matthew 12:

"It is your doctrine that Satan has possessed these whom I have cured. It is, also, your doctrine that he has helped me to cure them. If so, then he has helped me to undo what he had done. He has aided me to cast himself out. Christ was not satisfied by showing them the intrinsic absurdity of their argument. He showed them that it might as well be applied to them as to him." Barnes Commentary on Matthew 12:20-28.

"...in the conflict with Satan, neutrality is impossible." Wycliffe commentary, page 950.

Jane E. #7 was a woman who found deliverance from alcohol through a process. She began attending a recovery program and achieved sobriety. I knew her from attending the same groups but not much outside of that. After several years of sobriety, she asked to talk with me one night at a recovery meeting. She told of how she had acquired a deep resentment towards me that lasted quite a while. The source apparently was those "Jesus" shirts I wore on occasion. I had several that were either homemade or picked up at a Bible book store. One night she was praying about this resentment, asking God why she hated me so much. She was smiling while telling me this so I had no idea where it was going.

Then she said God spoke to her, telling her the reason she hated me was because "you forgot Me." Jane E. #7 had learned about Christ as a young teenager, but left Him behind for booze. Even with several years of God's grace in her life producing sobriety, she still had no room for Jesus. The reason she wanted to talk was to say thanks for wearing the shirts. The irritation drove her to God seeking freedom from the bitterness, and she found Christ. She was now going to church and had more peace in her heart than she knew was possible. The Father had led her to the Son.

CHAPTER SIX

12 Common Bonds
between Recovery and Church

1. No Earthly King
2. Self Governing Agents.
3. No Central Identification System
4. Individual Responsibility for Actions
5. Singular God, Multiple Names
6. Biblical Roots
7. Carrying the Message
8. Fellowship
9. Importance of the Newcomer
10. Power of Testimonies
11. Altruistic Emphasis
12. Singular Purpose

Our world is full of standards. Measurements, ethical concepts, scientific formulas, laws of physics, laws of the court, etc. All of these are used as a way to measure a variable against the standard to see if it holds up under close examination. One of most common is a simple tape measure. Several people could look at a piece of wood and have varying opinions of the length, but the use of a tape measure would verify the true length. As long as the tape measure was properly made according to the set standards, the truth would be known. The piece of wood could also be duplicated somewhere else by using the same standards of measurement. The purpose is to verify accuracy by having a method of comparing variables to a set standard.

The same principles are used for organizations everywhere. Rules and standards for operation are adopted either from pre-determined standards that cannot be changed, or from unique standards that the organization establishes. Some of these are flexible, others are not. The organization will run well if the standards are followed, especially if they were taken from sources proven to be successful. Changing the standards to fit unproven methods, or letting violations become the new standard, will only result in problems and chaos. Some changes can be made to adapt to varying conditions, but the core values of the proven standards must remain.

Manufacturing plants develop standards to ensure the product they make continues to be consistent over time. Not being able to follow the standard leads to problems, such as warranty claims and dissatisfied customers. The company will descend into compromise and chaos if the variations are not corrected. The product will eventually be different from the original intent. Companies spend a lot of time and effort to ensure consistency with their standards. They can make changes in their products to remain current with trends in the market, as long as the core standards remain consistent. Failure to adapt to the changing market will lead to the company's demise. Resting on the successes of yesterday, they will become ineffective in the current marketplace.

The Bible is God's standard by which we compare the variables of this world. It contains not only moral and doctrinal standards, but also guidelines for organizations that serve people. When an organization is set up according to the standards of God's Word, a successful future lies ahead. Blessings not yet realized will come to such an organization, as will failure if the standards are compromised. Changes can be made to adapt to the variables of cultures and people, as long as the core standards set by God are not compromised. Doing so will result in chaos.

Both churches and recovery programs are based on standards set forth in the Bible. These are historical and cultural facts. Yet today, some churches and recovery programs have varied so far from the standards that you can hardly recognize them from the original intent. Others have held to the standards so legalistically that they haven't been able to adapt to changes in culture and people. Rigid, legalistic, and "uncompromising" is their mantra. Yet they are just as far off track as those who abandoned the core values. They are ineffective in the world today, resting on yesterday's successes. Just being the opposite of what is wrong doesn't make you right.

Anytime a standard is compromised, the goal is to return to the standard, or at least it should be. I worked in a manufacturing plant for nearly 20 years, in departments for Maintenance, Projects, Engineering, Safety, and Quality Assurance. Over time, situations would arise where standards had been compromised. It was only by measuring or comparing the problem to the standard that a solution could be found. It wasn't always easy. People have a way of defending what they are doing based more on a perception than reality. Time has a way of altering people's memories. Some of these situations would have been comical if it weren't for the resulting chaos, but sometimes you just have to laugh, because there is no other sane response to the insanity.

When people run a church just by trying to do everything exactly the way it's always been done, then problems will arise. Mostly due to the fact that what people are comparing it to is more likely what their grandparents did than what Jesus taught. Statements about doing things the old fashioned way are a false standard, because nobody actually does them. If that's really the truth, then get rid of the pews, air conditioner, inside bathrooms and walk to church. The goal should be to keep the core values while adapting to cultural and ethnic influences. The message of salvation through Jesus Christ cannot be changed, but how people function as a body of Christ can. Recovery groups are functioning all over the world with the same core principles providing success while adapting to cultural and ethnic influences. Knowing the difference between a false standard and a real one is the challenge, as well as knowing which one can change and which one cannot.

When a storm is coming in the south, people run out and buy up all the milk and bread. Grocery stores will have full shelves of everything else, but the milk and bread areas are ravished. I grew up in earthquake country. Water, flashlights, and ready to eat foods were good to have on hand. But milk and bread? After many inquiries and still no solid answer as to why, it seems that severe storms in the south are cause for French Toast. Doing things the same as they have always been done does not always make sense, especially if you don't even know why you're doing it.

There are standards that were established to guide both of these institutions. Jesus gave quite a few of these guidelines for the church while on earth, and in fact He was the standard for the church of the New Testament. Despite this fact, it only took a few decades before the early churches were already off track. A lot of the writings of the apostle Paul in the New Testament are letters to churches addressing problems and giving direct counsel to correct them. In A.D. 49, Paul wrote to the church in Galatia: *"I am astonished that you are so quickly deserting the one who called you to live in the grace of Christ and are turning to a different gospel— which is really no gospel at all. Evidently some people are throwing you into confusion and are trying to pervert the gospel of Christ."* Galatians 1:6-7.

Other letters to the churches of that day had the same theme, correcting problems based on a departure from the standards. Not the standard customs or traditions of the Old Testament, which is what Paul addressed as a problem in the letter to the Colossians, but the standards Jesus set as the resurrected King. The Cross changed everything. It set new standards according to the progression of God's plan for the world. The core principles of the Old Testament were not changed, but fulfillment of these principles did cause change. Jesus clarified this himself when he said: *"Do not think that I have come to abolish the Law or the Prophets; I have not come to abolish them but to fulfill them."* Matthew 5:17.

Adjusting to changes in the world while keeping adherence to core standards is a challenge. Yet it is possible, as long as no violations of the core standards are made. But if violations exist and a return to the standards is not made, the organization will lose its resemblance of the original. As such, it would eventually become a counterfeit and ineffective. This is the common challenge that both churches and recovery programs have experienced. Just as the apostle Paul had to write documents to point out the errors, so did the original recovery program, Alcoholics Anonymous.

A.A.'s founding principles were based on Biblical core values. These are historical facts recorded in a variety of sources including some of A.A.'s approved literature. Yet, within a short period of time the program was drifting off track. The official date of A.A.'s beginning is June 10, 1935, and within 12 years of the program being formed it was necessary to develop the 12 Traditions. These core principles were established to correct problems that were either discovered after the program began, or to address issues arising from misuse of the core principles. By 1950, these 12 Traditions were officially adopted and have remained intact to this day. They have not completely prevented violations of the standards, but they have given a measuring tool, a tape measure of sorts, to compare any changes. This tool of measurement can be used anywhere to reproduce the same product that was originally intended, as long as the tool is used properly.

There were several issues arising for the early A.A. program, one of which had to do with the application of the term "God as we understood Him." The founding members of this program had developed a method of reaching drunks who were not only people of faith, but also agnostics and atheists. A method of recovery from alcoholism for anyone which included faith in God, amazing. To meet the obvious challenges, some methods that were given to A.A. by the Oxford Groups were changed, but still held true to the core Biblical values. The result was an effective model of recovery that was working, the 12 Steps, and true to human nature people immediately started violating the core standards. Just like people did in the early church not too long after Jesus went back to heaven.

Over a period of time, some recovery groups and other programs got so far from the original standards that concern arose from within. People developed the idea that God could be whatever you wanted Him to be, a door knob, a coffee cup, or whatever. In part it was this issue that drove the A.A. program to draft and adopt the 12 Traditions to correct error and try to preserve the program for future generations. The apostle Paul wrote several letters that are included in the New Testament for the same reasons. Correct error, and try to preserve the church. Of course it was God who guided Paul to write, just as He helped the founders of A.A. try to preserve the integrity of a God honoring Biblically rooted program. The 12 Traditions are not infallible, but they weren't the idea of some person with an agenda either. God will protect that which honors Him.

It is amazing how churches today set their own standards and call them Christian standards, whether it be methods of worship, styles of music, or certain clothes. For several decades, conservative churches have pushed the agenda that preachers have to wear ties and cannot wear colored shirts. Other Christians recognizing a false standard have rejected these concepts, because the Bible never taught such a thing. There is a myriad of other examples that are not worth mentioning. So where do they come from?

People make up standards that are supposed to be the way things have always been done, and everything else has to be measured by them. These false standards have been defended by people who think they are doing right by God. Just ask them. It would be funny if it weren't for the fact that so much chaos has been caused by people acting this way. Sometimes you just have to laugh, because there's no other sane response to the insanity. Maybe people who believe in the preacher/tie thing should dress in the pulpit like George Washington, because that is truly old fashioned!

It is also true that violation of a standard does not change the standard, just like a lie does not change the truth. The reason we know it's a lie is because we have the truth to compare it to. Sometimes it is necessary to look at the original concept of an institution to know if a current version is true to the standard, or if a new one has been created. There are many that claim to be right, comparison to the standard will verify their claim.

All recovery programs today have their origins in Alcoholics Anonymous. Many other programs have sprung from the success of A.A., and have addressed a host of issues that people struggle with. Some of these programs have written their own books, but the true standard of recovery is the "Big Book" of A.A., as it generically called. The program of recovery is recorded in the first 11 chapters. The rest are personal testimonies.

Some people think that Elvis Presley was the founder of rock and roll music, but even he pointed to Gospel music as the origins of rock and roll. Along with Elvis, people like Johnny Cash and Jerry Lee Lewis gave much credit for the roots of rock music to Sister Rosetta Tharpe, a black Gospel singer of the 1930's and 1940's. Her influence and innovative style of music inspired others. Sometimes to find the standard we have to go back to the original source, not just look at how we believe things have always been done. This is necessary when the current method is so far from the original that it's hard to recognize. It is difficult to see the Gospel in today's rock and roll, but not impossible. It depends on how the current version measures to the original standard and many artists today are producing God honoring music with rock, soul, blues, and other styles.

A.A.'s roots were in the Oxford Groups, a Christian organization trying to help alcoholics get sober. They had already developed the standards for a recovery program from the Bible. These were later changed and developed into the 12 Steps of A.A. without compromising the standards given by the Oxford Groups. Later in this chapter, we will look at why A.A. continued when the Oxford groups went away.

So the purpose of this chapter is to review the 12 Common Bonds between the church and recovery groups. These bonds are standards by which both of these institutions were originally based upon. Whether or not a current church or recovery group adheres to these standards doesn't change a thing, it only points out error and departure from the standards. Changing to adapt to the current world is not compromising, as long as the fundamental standards are upheld. It will be important to keep this in mind while reviewing these common bonds, most everyone knows of an example where these standards are being violated.

The 12 Common Bonds are not unique to just these two organizations; they exist in others that are religious or non-religious. But when all 12 are applied, it's hard to find another organization that will be left standing along with the church and recovery. Some can be eliminated on any one of these principles, others after a few, most if not all after 12. An Old Testament scripture states: *"A cord of three strands is not quickly broken."* Ecclesiastes 4:12.

If three makes it hard to break, then twelve makes it virtually unbreakable.

#1 - No Earthly King:

One significant event of the Old Testament is recorded in the book of I Samuel. In Chapter Eight a dialogue takes place between the prophet Samuel and the nation of Israel. Samuel is speaking for God as a divine messenger, and is asked by the people to petition God for a king, one that would rule over the nation of Israel. While there are many subjects to study from this account, the one that applies here is God's displeasure with the request. Even though Samuel warns of the consequences to come, Israel still insists on having an earthly king.

God's attitude with His people is spoken through Samuel in Chapter 12, when he tells Israel what an evil thing they did in asking for a king. It is obvious that God wants us to be directly connected to Him, and not put an earthly authority between Him and us. People today still make the same mistakes. *"And you will realize what an evil thing you did in the eyes of the* LORD *when you asked for a king."* 1 Samuel 12:17.

Recovery programs, however, do not have an earthly king. It is one of the strengths of these programs, one that has been studied by outside groups. It seems mystifying that such a large organization could function with no earthly king. But if we consider that it aligns with God's desires for the nation of Israel, then it makes perfect sense. This standard of A.A. has been so intriguing to people outside the program that major universities have commissioned studies to find out how this could be. It's really not a mystery; maybe they should just give their money to missionaries and read the Bible instead.

The 12 Traditions are the organizational standards for recovery programs. Tradition 2 states *"For our group purpose there is but one ultimate authority- a loving God as he may express himself in our group conscience. Our leaders are but trusted servants; they do not govern."* The concept of no human authority is consistent with God's displeasure with Israel. A.A. does not have a human authority that makes decisions for everyone; God expresses Himself through His people. A lot of churches state they are "congregationally ruled," meaning the members of the church collectively make decisions based on God's leading. Unfortunately, many churches do not actually operate by the standard they believe in. There are churches, however, that do adhere to the standard of having no earthly king, and those typically are healthy, vibrant, and growing.

This principle not only gives insights into why some churches eventually cease to exist, but also why the predecessor to A.A. is no longer around. The Oxford Groups were the organization that taught recovery to the co-founders of A.A. So where are the Oxford Groups today? In a word, gone. The cause may be debatable, but a glimpse is recorded in the book "Courage to Change" by Bill Pitman. It's a collection of letters and communications between several people who influenced the start of A.A. Indirectly, it records that the Oxford Groups had earthly kings.

The Reverend Sam Shoemaker was a person who had a lot of interaction with Bill Wilson, A.A. co-founder. Bill was frequently urged by the Oxford groups to become involved in evangelism. But his God given desire was to help alcoholics, so he had to go against the tide to do God's will. A letter wrote to Bill years later by Rev. Shoemaker stated that the Oxford Groups believed that anything not done under the supervision of the group was as good as not done at all, a position that Rev. Shoemaker called an error in his letter. The groups were a system of control.

The Oxford groups were structured, a hierarchy of sorts with ranks and persuasive votes. Individuals within the Oxford program were given titles that were military ranks, such as Lieutenant. In short, the Oxford Groups had earthly kings. They controlled the organization and insisted that anyone coming into their program follow the rules. The Oxford Groups withdrew into Britain in 1938 and changed the name to "Moral Re-Armament" (MRA). While much can be said about the history and influence of the Oxford Groups on the forming of A.A., the fact is that one organization remained and the other one did not.

There are times when events line up to give us a glimpse of God at work. Sometimes it's obvious, other times it takes a little more focus to see. Occasionally, a curious series of events produces that glimpse. The earliest attempts to curb alcohol abuse in America started before it was even a nation, as early as 1750 with repeated failed attempts. The first state prohibition was in Maine in 1851, and in 13 states by 1855. It continued to be enough of a problem that in the early 1900's the U.S. and several other countries passed laws of prohibition. In January 1919, the 18th Amendment of the U.S. Constitution went into effect. The earthly king of the U.S. Government was taking action. The result was the roaring 20's.

God has given man a free will to use or abuse, our choice. When prohibition tried to control people, they simply refused and put a lot of creativity into getting around the rules. As the legal attempts to control man's will failed, one by one, countries repealed their prohibition laws. Canada and Hungary (1919), Sweden (1922), Russia (1925), Norway (1927), Finland (1932), and Iceland (1933). The U.S. was the last, which took place in December of 1933. One year later, in December of 1934, Bill Wilson took his last drink. Centuries of trying to make people behave through an earthly king, and when the king stepped down, God stepped in. What succeeded was a program that taught people to surrender to God, apply His standards, and be directly accountable to Him. No earthly king, and not only did it work right away, but it continues to work throughout the world today.

#2 - Self Governing Agents:

Having no earthly king is only half the goal. It is not enough to state what you do not want to be. Completing the picture means determining what you will be. It is clearly God's intention for us to be self governing, agents of His kingdom on earth. But humans like to control other humans, and even though both churches and recovery programs were established on the idea of being guided by our conscience as directed by God, control creeps in.

In the 2nd Tradition established by A.A., is the term "a loving God as He expresses Himself in our group conscience." The concept here is a group of individuals who are directly serving God, people that are surrendered to His divine will. Together they can make decisions so that no one can make a false claim of speaking on God's behalf. Otherwise it would be like having those people who claim to "whisper" to animals. How do we know if they're right or wrong? There's no one to verify their statements as they set and measure their own standards.

This principle also keeps organizations out of the control of certain humans who would try to use it for personal gain. Churches that become controlled by certain individuals ultimately lose focus on lost souls and wind up in church disputes over minor issues, or become a cult type atmosphere far from the original standard. Recovery groups can do the same, losing focus on helping addicts and falling into disputes over insignificant issues. Both will remain healthy and effective if they take their self governing responsibility seriously. The organization establishes the standards, but the individual is responsible to God for their actions. Self governing agents express the love of God into a world that needs hope, as directed by God Himself.

"The only thing that counts is an expression of love. For in Christ Jesus neither circumcision nor uncircumcision has any value.

The only thing that counts is faith expressing itself through love."
Galatians 5:6.

This is really why the Big Book states that the ultimate purpose of recovery is to have a clear conscience before God and man. Without it, an addict's life will become chaos, which is why Paul wrote in his first letter to Timothy that not having a clear conscience could shipwreck his faith. And whose responsibility is it to clean up the conscience? It's ours, individually, not as a group or by forced submission. We cannot be self governing agents without a clear conscience.

God gave us the standard of keeping our conscience clear, and we are individually responsible for the action. We do not clean up someone else's conscience, and no one cleans up ours. We do it because we want to, because we believe in God and accept His wisdom. In the process, we learn to be governed by conscience, one that is clean and right with God.

#3 - No Central Identification System:

Most churches have a list, the ever evasive, never defined, always changing, Church Membership List. It has to be one of the most inaccurate documents on earth. For example, trying to determine what constitutes a "member" can be challenging to say the least. The parts about believing in God and Jesus Christ are pretty simple, but then we have baptism, attendance, serving, tithing, etc. When the congregation gets ready to vote on something important, the question will come up, "who can vote?" Well, a member, but only ones in good standing, whatever that means. And over the age of 18, or perhaps 16. And must have attended church once in let's say the last 30 days, maybe 60, unless they're in the hospital or on vacation. Get the point? It is totally evasive and completely subjective. I once heard a deacon respond to this question by saying "Can't count the spirits."

People try to determine who is saved, who is not, who "really" knows God, who does not. It is truly amazing that anyone would even try such an exercise of insanity. Even when the outward appearance seems to point away from God, can we really look into the soul of a person?

What this really points to is the fact that the only true church membership list is in Heaven, called the Lamb's Book of Life. It belongs to Christ, and it's not available to check out. Churches make a legitimate attempt to have a membership list, but in all honesty they would have to admit it's more of a contact list for calls and mailing. The best we can do cannot be confirmed.

Recovery groups are the same in this regard. Anonymity is one of the core standards of A.A., enough so that it's in the name. There is no official membership list, no central identification system, yet the estimates worldwide number in the millions. Most groups have a phone list so members can contact each other for support, but the only possibility of a record would exist in Heaven, or at least in God's memory since He is all knowing.

Membership in both of these institutions is also a personal choice. There is no forced membership, at least not in those adhering to the proper standards. Keeping membership as a choice protects the access for all people, the same as the Gospel is intended to be. In many cultures or religions an individual has a pre-determined membership awaiting them. Some will even kill their own family for a violation. Neither church nor recovery programs would do this just because you wanted to join another organization.

This principle overlaps considerably with other common bonds, such as having No Earthly King (#1) and Individual Responsibility for Actions (#4). Perhaps the reason God doesn't allow people to have this information is because they would use it for control and greed, especially when these already take place without the book. Violations do not change the standard. They only point out error. Churches and recovery groups that keep this in mind seem to do well in Carrying the Message (#7).

#4 - Individual Responsibility for Actions:

Recovery calls for complete ownership of individual actions, both current and past. The 12 Step process is designed to resolve the wrongs of the past by owning and reconciling what an addict has done. The Big Book describes a person as "a tornado roaring his way through the lives of others." It goes on to address the concept of full ownership of the destruction caused, stating that mere sobriety isn't enough. "He is like the farmer who came out of his cyclone cellar to find his home ruined. To his wife, he remarked, "Don't see anything the matter here, Ma. Ain't it grand the wind stopped blowin?" (pg 82). At the very core of 12 Step recovery is individual responsibility for actions. Those who treat recovery as a "feel good" experience do so by ignoring the damage they've done to others. They're just happy the wind stopped blowing, and most of them typically relapse.

The Bible calls for ownership of faults and offers reconciliation and restitution as the method to resolve those wrongs. Jesus taught that even if you're at the altar to worship God and remember that you have a problem with another person, to go and take care of it first, then come and offer your gift to God (Matthew 5:23-24). True Christianity requires people to take individual responsibility for their actions and resolve conflicts with others. The founders of A.A. were taught these principles by Christians, who understood the life or death need for alcoholics to have peace with God and man. Imagine how churches could be transformed with this sense of urgency when it comes to conflicts within the body of Christ. The motivation is lost without the desperation of an addict, but it can be re-gained individually.

Most of the other religions in the world have a variety of ways to resolve wrongdoings, for cleansing or pardon based on works, to make God happy or appease His anger. Examples are endless. The Russian Orthodox Church has an annual ritual that takes place in January. People line up for a church sponsored three dip rinse cycle in freezing cold water. Its purpose for each person is to obtain pardon for the previous year's sins. In India, every seven years a certain group of people make a pilgrimage to a river to wash. On the big day, the procession into the water is led by a large number of naked men, with ceremonial face painting. It also serves as atonement for wrongs done.

The point here is not to invalidate these or other practices, but simply point out that Biblical practices are vastly different from those of other religions. God's divine plan for personal responsibility is often set aside for a repetitive ritual, one that has nothing to do with conscience or harm done to others. Rarely do our actions only affect us, tornadoes cause widespread damage. The farther an individual or nation gets away from the Bible, the less accountable they become for their choices, which are easily dismissed by a ritual. In other cases, the religion justifies violence, and even rewards its patrons for taking the lives of others. Christianity and recovery have common bonds in the area of personal responsibility for actions, and are vastly different from other religions and institutions.

Our world today has a common problem, false victimization, which is the process of a perpetrator becoming a victim. It's accomplished by blaming a person, place, or situation for personal actions. People seek compensation payments for being false victims, passing off their personal responsibility to anything but themselves. Someone didn't put up a sign, write a warning label, or have the fortune telling ability to predict what someone else was going to do. There is no acceptance of personal responsibility for decisions that lead to actions. False acceptance of God's will is expressed in a law suit. The impact hits us all, damaging the economic structure of an entire nation. The process of America being a victimized society is the process of accepting false religions. It is selfish and self centered.

In 2001, the Senate Commerce Committee rejected the President's nomination for the head the Consumer Product Safety Commission, Mary Sheila Gall. Political motives by one party led to the nomination being declined because she had the courage to say that people are responsible for how they use products. What a concept! While the real motives were party driven, a good candidate was de-railed because the idea of holding someone accountable for their actions was ridiculed. It seems that even the Consumer Protection Agency has trouble holding people responsible for their own actions.

Eventually education became the focus, the key to all answers. But when education is the key then personal responsibility is absent. The idea is "if you didn't teach me, then I'm not responsible." False victims line up to play the education card. Huge law suits are centered on the level of training provided by a company to its employees. If a person sexually harasses another co-worker, the focus is on the company's training methods and documentation. The employer becomes responsible for the individual actions of its employees, when all they did was provide a job.

I was personally involved in a discussion at the manufacturing plant where I worked, which focused on why a lot of our employees were obviously abusing alcohol. One manager asked, "What are we doing to these guys that is causing them to drink like this?" My response, "giving them a job." What they did with their paycheck was their responsibility, and while I would have been the first in line to help anyone get sober, I was not willing to accept responsibility for anyone's decision to use their paycheck to stay drunk. It was not a popular response with the other managers. Corporate America is full of false victims who blame the company for their actions.

Acceptance of the will of our divine Creator is the right solution. There is no doubt that God offers us answers to life's problems, but He doesn't force those answers on us. We have to choose. There are basically two paths to take, self-will and God's will. One takes us away from God; the other towards Him. When a person takes individual responsibility for their actions, and chooses to resolve wrongdoings through Biblical solutions, the result is a life at peace with God and man. A.A. states in the Big Book that the ultimate purpose of the recovery program is to have a clear conscience before God and others. A principle that was not only learned from Christianity, but is also as common to both organizations as it is uncommon to others.

"*When a man's ways please the LORD, He makes even his enemies to be at peace with him.*" Proverbs 16:7 (NKJV).

#5 - Singular God, Multiple Names:

The different religions in the world today and throughout history are numerous, and so are the differences in how they describe God. To decide what is correct and what is false, a standard has to be used. One that is proven over time, is trustworthy, and can be repeated in any location. The Bible is the Word of God, inspired by our Creator to describe Himself to us, so we do not have to use our imagination. It is the standard, and describes God as a singular being having three personalities in the Father, Son, and Holy Spirit, but still one. This factor creates a clear distinction between Christianity and most every other religion or organization centered on God. "*For there are three that bear witness in heaven: the Father, the Word, and the Holy Spirit; and these three are one.*" I John 5:7 (NKJV).

For some people their concept of God is very limited, or tainted by an image that resembles a person rather than a deity. This is true for churches and recovery, because people who are new to these organizations typically come with baggage. If a person was abused by someone calling themselves a Christian, their belief in God will be affected. Either way, these people will eventually come to terms with the limitations of their beliefs. Simply put, if your God isn't big enough to love, care, and provide for you, then trade him in for a bigger one. Not one from an imagination or a human system, but the One who wrote the standard. One with all wisdom and all power, singular and personal.

The term used for a singular God is "monotheism." Many of the religions throughout history have been "polytheistic," meaning they have multiple gods. The ancient Greeks are said to have had 30,000 gods, one for just about everything. The apostle Paul used this culture to point to the one true God by speaking about a shrine the Greeks had to "the unknown God." Paul told them in Acts 17 that the God who was unknown to them was the "creator of Heaven and Earth." In other words, Paul dismissed the other 30,000 gods and stated undeniably that God is singular. He tried to get them to trade their gods in for a singular, all sufficient God.

God as He is described in the A.A.'s Big Book is singular. He has various names, just at the Bible does, but never described in terms of polytheism. One of the phrases read at every A.A. meeting states, "There is One who has all power--that One is God, may you find Him now." Not only is God referenced as singular, but the word "one" is capitalized both times in this phrase, because He is One. Sometimes we have to search for hidden truth, other times it is in plain view.

In the previous chapter, we looked at the 3rd Step prayer from the Big Book, which also applies to where Paul is talking about the Greek shrine to the unknown god. Throughout the Big Book God is referred to by many names, yet always capitalized to declare that He is not an unknown God, He is God. The writers of the Big Book fully intended that the reader would come to know the same God who inspired the words of the Bible.

Part of the 3rd Step prayer states "Take away my difficulties, that victory over them may bear witness to those I would help of Thy Power, Thy Love, and Thy Way of life." In this prayer the words Power, Love, and Way are capitalized, pointing to names of God. From the Bible we know that:

- We receive the Power of the Holy Spirit in our lives.
- God is Love, so much so that He (the Father) gave His only Son.
- Jesus said, "I am the Way, the Truth, and the Life; no man comes to the Father, but by Me."

In the Bible, Jesus refers to Himself as the "Way," and in the Big Book the word "Way" capitalized. The 3rd Step prayer points us to the Trinity, and to the Son of God. In recovery and Christianity, we serve a God who has a name, the name above all names. His name is Jesus, and it's referenced in this recovery prayer.

One of the common objections by Christians towards recovery leads to the use of the word "nebulous." It's a word Christians use to describe the God of recovery. By definition it means "lacking definite form, shape, or content; vague." Unfortunately, the people I've encountered using this word are some of the worst violators of contempt prior to investigation. They have no idea what they're talking about, but heard something from somebody who is a Christian so it must be true. They compare recovery to a cult, but religious cults take away the deity of God, recovery does not.

The Bible teaches a singular God with many names and descriptions, such as Jehovah, King of Kings, Lord of Lords, Lion of Judah, Prince of Peace, Adonai (Master), and simply "I AM." The Big Book of A.A. also teaches a singular God with many names and descriptions, such as Creator, Father of Light, Maker, Him who has all knowledge and all power, the Spirit, and others. God in the Big Book is masculine, never described as feminine, same as the Bible. No mother earth. But there is one name used in recovery that draws more attention than any other, Higher Power.

The misuse of this term has caused controversy. Using the term higher power did not give people the permission to make up a god that fit their opinion, it simply provided a name that pointed out two important characteristics of God. First, His ways are higher than our ways, and second, His power is greater than ours or anything on earth. This was the concept of the original standard, despite what anyone in Christianity or recovery might say. Compromise doesn't change the standard; it only makes the violations obvious.

It is safe to say that anytime God is the subject with humans, controversy is close by. The name Higher Power disturbs Christians, the name of Jesus disturbed the Jews, not much has changed in 2,000 years. A sample of A.A. 's own approved literature makes a strong connection. It was approved in 1970 at an A.A. International Conference, and has been incredibly popular ever since. It is named, "A Member's Eye View" (Pages 26-27):

This coming Sunday, in the churches of many of us, there will be read that portion of the Gospel of Matthew which recounts the time when John the Baptist was languishing in the prison of Herod, and, hearing of the works of his cousin Jesus, he sent two of his disciples to say to Him, "Art thou He who is to come, or shall we look for another?" And Christ did as He so often did. He did not answer them directly, but wanted John to decide for himself. And so He said to the disciples: "Go and report to John what you have heard and what you have seen: the blind see, the lame walk, the lepers are cleansed, the deaf hear, the dead rise, the poor have the gospel preached to them." Back in my childhood catechism days, I was taught that the "poor" in this instance did not mean only the poor in a material sense, but also meant the "poor in spirit," those who burned with an inner hunger and an inner thirst; and that the word "gospel" meant quite literally the good news. More than 16 years ago, four men—my boss, my physician, my pastor, and the one friend I had left—working singly and together, maneuvered me into A.A. Tonight, if they were to ask me, "Tell us, what did you find?" I would say to them what I now say to you: "I can tell you only what I have heard and seen: It seems the blind do see, the lame walk, the lepers are cleansed, the deaf hear, the dead rise, and over and over again, in the middle of the longest day or the darkest night, the poor in spirit have the good news told to them." God grant that it may always be so.

If you seek the Father, you will find the Son.

#6 - Biblical Roots:

Besides the connection to Christian groups in the forming of A.A., there are several scriptural principles that were applied to the way alcoholics were to help other alcoholics. Once these principles were established, the result was exponential growth.

One of these was to walk away from a person who did not want help. This was taught by Jesus, who said that if you are not welcomed, then leave and "shake the dust off your feet." When early A.A.'s would go to the hospital to visit a struggling drunk, they would tell their stories and ask if the person wanted what they had to offer. If the drunk said no, they left. Jesus was teaching how to share the Gospel with others, the Good News, and He said if they didn't want to hear it, move on. You might say Jesus was a mover and a shaker, so move your feet and shake 'em if you need to.

Another Biblical root is the connection between the Great Commission and the recovery model of "Carrying the Message." Jesus gave the instructions at the end of the book of Matthew to "go into all the world" with the message of hope. Early A.A.'s did not have meetings, they had to "go" to the hospital and find drunks to work with. They were motivated, and didn't sit around waiting for people to find them. Somehow over time, recovery programs drifted into a cliché of "being here when they're ready," meaning attending meetings and waiting for drunks to come in. The qualification for this approach is often quoted from the 11th Tradition, which speaks about "attraction rather than promotion." The problem is the rest of that tradition is addressing the public relations policy for press, radio, and films. It is intended to prevent someone from using a public format to speak for A.A. and try to attract people to come. How easy it is to get off track.

If the co-founders and early members of A.A. had waited for drunks to show up, we wouldn't have recovery programs. It is not Biblical and it would not have worked. But how many Christians are sitting in church on Sunday waiting for lost souls to show up? Jesus said "go," and He meant what He said. Vibrant, healthy, exciting churches "go" into their communities and reach out to people. The same is true of recovery programs. The healthy ones are involved in communities by going into "Hospitals and Institutions" (H&I). What other organizations besides these two are going into all the world with their message? And having success based on Biblical principles?

God has a way of moving people around to fulfill his work. For some it seems to happen in the late 40's, about the time you're getting settled in and ready to coast into retirement. This happened in our lives when God called my wife and I to move across the U.S. to a much different culture than what we were used to. The purpose was to continue our work with people and families struggling with addictions. California was quite different than the Bible belt where we moved to.

One of the first things apparent in our new area was the amount of sympathy being given to addicts by the families and the culture in general. Empathy can help, altruism is necessary, but sympathy? No way. Addicts love sympathy, but it's the last thing they need. It promotes self pity, and typically motivates the families to pursue the addicts to the point of enabling.

One day I got a call from Jewel E. #2, who said she had an adult son and an adult grandson sitting around her house drinking beer all day. She wanted to know if I would come over and talk with them. I declined, but I did say that if she gave them my phone number and they called and asked for help, then I would do anything I could. I wasn't going to chase them. There is a proper balance between "going" and "leaving." Besides, when I asked who owned the house and she confirmed it was her, it became time to ask some other questions about these boys. Such as how were they getting food and a dry bed to sleep on. You can't violate God's principles and get a blessing. These men were not reaping what they were sowing, and according to Galatians 6, they should have been experiencing some consequences. Going the extra mile is a short term response, not a daily lifestyle. These recovery principles are deeply rooted in the Bible.

Peter and John had a message to get out. If they had violated the Lord's directions, they would have had no success. One day both of these men and their message were confirmed by an evil influence and a wise man. They were brought before the religious council to be punished. But one man spoke up, Gamaliel.

"Therefore, in the present case I advise you: Leave these men alone! Let them go! For if their purpose or activity is of human origin, it will fail. But if it is from God, you will not be able to stop these men; you will only find yourselves fighting against God." Acts 5:38-39.

Maybe one of the strongest proofs of the Biblical roots of A.A. is its exponential growth and utter inability to stop it. There are other religions beside Christianity that have experienced these two characteristics, but none have the ability to help any person in any culture around the world with any problem they might have. Only Christianity and recovery have this impact throughout the world. Most non-Christian religions primarily help their own people with very little influence to cross ethnic or cultural barriers.

On one of the mission trips I took to Russia, I was asked to speak about addictions with a young priest from the Russian Orthodox Church. I left that decision with the local pastor since I was there to help his church start a recovery program. He said it would be fine, so we moved forward. When the priest showed up he walked in with a camera crew, so we knew he was serious about what he was doing. He was also trying to help with the problems in their city, which had approximately 500,000 people with an estimated 50% addicted to drugs and alcohol. You could see its influence everywhere. Just imagine if 50% of the people in the town or city you live in were addicted. You would see it everywhere.

One of the questions he asked was "how do you know the 12 Step recovery process is from God?" Speaking through a translator can be challenging. Keeping the information simple is best, you really learn how much of our language is spoken in slang when someone is interpreting for you. I went to the simplicity of the principle being described here, that only a process from God could work for any culture on any problem, the same as the Gospel. We discussed the Biblical roots of 12 Step recovery. It was a great discussion, nothing was lost in the translation, and the priest was more than satisfied with the answer.

Many of the false religions of the world were started by a person despising mankind and finding "God," then becoming a messenger of a message that contradicts the Bible. They write a new Gospel, which is really no Gospel at all. A.A. did not write a new Gospel, it received its influence from the original one. The Cleveland Central Committee of A.A. distributed a pamphlet about "The Four Absolutes" of the Oxford Groups. It is another source of information clarifying the standards by which A.A. was formed, and documents that early compromises were taking place. The Foreword states *"The Four Absolutes are not a formal part of the A.A. philosophy of life. Since this is true, some may claim the Absolutes should be ignored. This premise is approximately as sound as it would be to suggest that the Bible should be scuttled."*

In writings about the Four Absolutes, author Dick B. points to the source as a book titled "The Principles of Jesus" by Dr. Robert E. Speer. He goes on to say that Dr. Speer believed the four principles were the "uncompromising moral standards taught by Jesus." So what were these standards: honesty, purity, unselfishness, and love. They played a significant role in what eventually became the 12 Steps of Recovery.

Lastly, new age philosophies teach that man is a product of evolution or a sudden accident while church and recovery teach we are a product of our loving Creator. Christianity works around the world for all people. Recovery as well not only cuts through cultural and ethnic boundaries, it also crosses into an unlimited amount of human problems. Nothing but God's Word empowered by His Spirit can accomplish such results. God's ways are higher than man's, and He won't contradict His own Word. The Biblical roots of 12 Step Recovery are visible throughout the world in the lives of broken people as they are restored through a relationship with their Heavenly Father.

#7 - Carrying the Message:

The message of the Gospel is God's love expressed to mankind, a message of hope and redemption. It is a message that He wants everyone to hear. Yet in the Bible there is a distinction drawn between the Jews and the Gentiles. In its simplest terms all mankind is either a Jew or Gentile.

The great news that came in the New Testament was that salvation was for the Gentiles as well as the Jews. This was not a popular message for some people who rejected the idea. But God will get His message out to the masses with or without the help of His people. When the Jews resisted, He went to the Gentiles.

While the depth of this subject can be left to the debaters, there is a simple application which points us to a common bond between Christianity and recovery. In the book Eternity in their Hearts, author Don Richardson calls attention to the lack of zeal by the Jews to deliver God's message, leaving God's people less motivated to pass their blessings on to "all people." God initially gave the message to the Jews, but eventually to the Gentiles because His people would not do His will.

In the same manner God initially gave the message of recovery to Christians, the Oxford Groups eventually gave it to some drunks to get the message out. The Rev. Sam Shoemaker had the message, but God transferred it to Bill Wilson. Gentiles were despised, and so were drunks. The Jews own religious belief system could not accept or change the message, so they just rejected it completely. Unfortunately, the same problem existed in the 1930's, and continues today. The church in general has rejected the message of recovery in the same way the Jews rejected the message of the Gospel. Not understanding that recovery is from God, there has been a lack of zeal to carry the message to all people. So, God had to give the message to a despised group to get it to the world. In the 1930's, you could lose your job if someone knew you were a drunk, which is why A.A. was established as an anonymous program. God chose the undesirable to reach the unreachable, and the result was uncontainable.

The common bond in carrying the message is shown in both the success and failure of church and recovery. Anytime you put imperfect people together to help other imperfect people, problems will arise. This usually happens when the standards which established the organization are compromised. The solution is returning to the standard, not creating new ones.

Some of the common church errors in carrying the message of the Gospel are:

- Waiting for people to show up at church to share the message.
- Becoming more of a social club for activities and entertainment.
- Expecting some of the people to do all of the work.
- Religious systems become more important than the people hurting.
- Christianity of comfort.
- The old guard protecting the church from change.

Some of the common 12 Step errors in carrying the message of recovery are:

- Waiting for people to show up at meetings to share the message.
- Becoming more of a social club for talking about insignificant issues.
- Expecting some of the people to do all of the work.
- 12 Traditions become more important than reaching alcoholics/addicts.
- Feel good program of comfort.
- Old timers protecting the program from change.

What would have happened if Paul had stayed in one place waiting for lost souls to come to him?

What would have happened if Bill Wilson and Dr. Bob had sat at Bob's house waiting for drunks to show up?

The errors also point to the common bonds. Both church and recovery were originally designed by God to go out into the world and find hurting people who needed hope. And in some locations both have evolved into a philosophy of "we'll be here when they're ready." If the only contact you have with lost souls and drunks is when they show up at your location, then you have compromised the standards established by God. "Go" is the command into "all" the world. God's hope doesn't sit in a building waiting for someone to show up. It "goes." And if certain people won't carry it, He will get someone else.

It is not uncommon at all to hear people in recovery quote the 11th Tradition when talking about carrying the message. "It's attraction rather than promotion" is the mantra. But this doesn't hold up under the worst of circumstances and is definitely contempt prior to investigation. Going out to where drunks are has nothing to do with press, radio, TV, or films. The 11th Tradition was created to protect A.A. from being represented in the media by one individual, nothing more, nothing less. Anytime "experts" take to the media speaking about 12 Step Recovery, damage results. People who don't know about recovery believe these people know what they're talking about, and are quick to accept anything they say as truth.

There's actually something for churches to learn from recovery in carrying the message. How much damage is caused by people going to the media as spokespersons for all of Christianity? There may be no way to really answer the question other than to say churches should consider adapting the same principles of the 11th Tradition. Using media to get the message of the Gospel out to the world is different than using it for self glorification. There is nothing wrong with the method or adapting to changes in technology to further the spread of the message, but there is something wrong when the attention is drawn to the person instead of God and the message.

Churches and recovery programs have a history of great success when they stay true to the standards, adapting to changes in the world without compromising the core principles. Some of the common successes in carrying the message of the Gospel and recovery are:

- Priorities in order: God, the Suffering, then the Servants.
- People of every nation and tongue working together.
- Acceptance of difficult people without judgment.
- The message is more important than the method.
- Able to change while keeping core values.
- An invisible source of strength working through visible people.
- Money is just a tool, it's ink on paper.
- The majority of workers are volunteers.
- A safe place that people run to, not from.

It's a testimony to the power of the Gospel when Christians of different denominations work together while maintaining their individual methods of worship. People are often too worried about only working with people of "like order and faith." Meanwhile, people die of addiction and lost souls spend eternity without God. If you find a church or recovery group that is effectively carrying the message, you will also find one that is willing to work with people who are different, because the focus is on getting the message out.

The Bible tells us that nothing can separate us from God's love. His power can move mountains, change history, and bring empires to their knees. It can part an ocean, shake the earth, and ride on the winds. Even the forces of evil cannot stop it. Yet there is one thing that can prevent His power from flowing into the world, a selfish heart. God delivers His message to the world through people. He could have written the Bible without humans, but he used them anyway. He can certainly find another person if we resist, but that doesn't change the fact that our own selfishness can prevent His power from flowing through us. Silence when we need to speak, bitterness when we need to love, and fear when we need to trust. These will choke off the message. He transferred the messages of the Gospel and recovery to the next in line, but only because the first choices stumbled over themselves. Oh, how He loves us, and we can show our love for Him through obedience to His will. "Thy will, not mine, be done."

Jesus worked with all kinds of people, experienced discomfort, and went where the people were. Sometimes He went completely out of his way to help someone, other times He went to the place where the religious were gathered to deliver a message. Either way, He was on the move and shaking feet. Carrying the message is not a subject of convenience, it never has been.

The call came. It was about 6:00 at night when my phone rang. During that period of my life I was working two jobs, which sometimes required back to back eight hour shifts. Work had started at midnight the previous night for one job, and continued in the morning for the second. Now I was home after a very long and exhausting day, getting ready to go to bed.

On the other end of the phone was a female friend who was in a panic. Another woman in our church, Jewel E. #3, was a single woman who found out she was pregnant, and was going to have an abortion. I was being asked to "go" with the caller to Jewel E. #3's home in the hope of changing her mind. James 1:27 says *"Religion that God our Father accepts as pure and faultless is this; to look after the orphans and widows in their distress, and to keep oneself from being polluted by the world."* What would you do? Throw the first stone? Practice righteous indignation? Love like Jesus? Honestly, would you stick to the rules or go? There were obvious problems with boundaries in this situation, but a life was on the line.

It was not a convenient time to go, but I went. Several months later a beautiful baby boy was born, and Jewel E. #3 had the courage to ask me to stand with her during her baby's dedication ceremony at our church. She gave our pastor permission to share her testimony, which he did. It was an incredibly powerful moment in God's House, and she was embraced and loved by the Body of Christ. Today, that little baby has become a grown man. God's power flowing through us into the world is a humbling experience, because we realize all we do is surrender. He does the rest.

Carry the message, whenever, wherever, God says to "go." He wants us to be the hands and feet of the message, so move and shake. God searches the world looking for willing servants to carry His message.

#8 – Fellowship:

We are created for fellowship. God put within us the fundamental desire for having relationships with other people and Him. This universal instinct within humans was the decision of an Omniscient God. And no other instinct within us causes more damage and destruction in our lives than this one. A vast majority of addicts who give up their recovery to get high again do so over relationships. Satan knows this all too well, and uses it to cause pain and suffering. Having the right relationships with people is part of having a right relationship with God, and vice versa.

Isolation is one aspect of addiction that kills. As such, physical attendance at recovery groups is essential to success. Isolation will also kill a child of God's faith. People get offended, bitter, hurt, then run and hide. God's will is not to live in isolation. We need to be connected to Him and other people.

While working to establish a recovery group in one city in Russia, I was corresponding by e-mail to weekly questions within the group. On one occasion, the group wanted to know if they should kick someone out who had relapsed and got drunk. The answer was to let them back in, which didn't connect well with the authority driven culture in Russia. The next question: how many times do you let them back in? We can thank Peter for helping us with that one, seventy times seven (Matthew 18:22). Not satisfied with that answer, the next question was to inquire as to the recommended method of punishment for the person who drank. Simple answer: none. Welcome them back with love and encouragement. The group was trying to isolate themselves from the addict, God's standards lead us out of isolation, and will correct cultural violations.

If you're really not sure about why fellowship is so important, just find a hermit, a real one. One time while camping in the Redwoods of northern California we came across the preserved habitat of the "Hendy Hermit," titled so for the Hendy Woods park that he lived adjacent to. Mr. H. had departed this life some time before, but one of his bungalows was still standing with a picture of him close by. What got my attention was the facial expression in his picture, pretty much on the severely crazy side. We are not created for isolation, pursuing it leads to instability.

There is a popular belief floating around that we can have fellowship with God without having fellowship with His people. The world can be your church. But this doesn't hold up under the worst of circumstances, and only has the appearance of sounding good. For one, it's a violation of scripture which is our standard to live by. Second, how does someone find you when they need help? The hyper-spiritual answer that God will miraculously bring everyone together outside the church does not work. Being a visible body of Christ is important. God chose to answer the problem of sin by sending His Son to be visible and make contact with other humans. He chose to come down to earth in human form where people could see Him. It's our example to live by.

So it is with recovery. A visible group ready to help people find sobriety. The concept of one addict doing for another what no one else can do, a fundamental principle of recovery. The same as one sinner helping another to find Jesus Christ. So why do some Christians and addicts try to go it alone, saying their connection to God is all they need, that involvement with people is optional? There's nothing in God's word or the Big Book to support such an approach. In fact, the scriptures say in Galatians 6 to "*Carry each other's burdens, and in this way you will fulfill the law of Christ.*" The concept is a weight that is too heavy for the person to carry alone, one that exceeds their personal abilities. So much for "*God will never give you more than you can handle,*" which would violate the law of Christ. He does give us more than we can handle, which is why He wants us to help each other, and why we need to avoid isolation. God's plan includes a visible body of His people who are ready to help carry burdens.

A safe environment is the standard for churches and recovery groups. So why do churches foster isolation of leaders with problems? Because it's not safe for them to expose themselves, most likely afraid they will be crucified. This causes great damage to the person and Christianity, because people stay sick and act out in other ways. It's no wonder the church has so many leaders who have fallen over problems with sex. Trying to hide a problem only increases the chance you will be exposed at a public level, and chaos is the result.

God intends for His earthly institutions to be a safe place for suffering people. The guiding principles of recovery groups, the standards, are there to ensure a safe environment for people who are full of pain and fear. Churches are compared to hospitals for sinners, and it was certainly Jesus mission to set this in motion. If a recovery group becomes unsafe for people to find help, then people will stop coming or avoid it altogether. Is church any different?

Sometime in the mid 1990's a man walked into the church I was attending, a homeless man. He was dirty, smelled, and stood out in the crowd. I watched for a moment after he walked in the sanctuary and noticed an uncomfortable look on his face. He turned around quickly and walked out, so I followed him and asked if he wanted to stay. He said it was obvious people didn't want him there. Even if he was already defensive, it didn't negate what some people did. The rejection was plain to see. Our pastor also saw it from the front of the church. He later commented that the "pillars of the Church fell."

I went outside with this man and sat down on the sidewalk by the street. It was winter and I actually sat on my Bible because the concrete was so cold. We talked for a bit, and after a while I invited him to come in with me, which he did. A church needs to be a safe place for difficult people to walk into and feel safe. Acceptance is something that people in general are sensitive to, especially if they've been hurt. A common response to recovery groups is when people say it is the first time they feel "a part of instead of apart from."

The importance of fellowship is more than obligation to a scripture in Hebrews. It is essential to reaching hurting people. It is a common bond in the success of both church and recovery.

#9 - Importance of the Newcomer:

Most organizations survive on the importance of the long term member or the one with the highest level of success. CEO's, Generals and Admirals, Presidents, etc. But the church and recovery have a common emphasis on the new person. Jesus emphasized this several times saying he came to serve not to be served, that the greatest among us is the servant of all. In recovery programs the term is "newcomer," and they are the most important people in the program. This standard was established by A.A. in its forming, a Biblical principle that has been key to its exponential success. Churches that maintain this standard do well in reaching the lost for Christ. When it gets turned upside down, chaos arises.

The 12 Traditions used in recovery programs serve to hold this standard in check. Tradition #2, which states that a loving God is the ultimate authority, goes on to say that "*our leaders are but trusted servants; they do not govern.*" Also, Tradition #9 states that groups "*may create service boards or committees directly responsible to those they serve.*" These principles point authority to God, and responsibility of service on the long term members to serve the new ones. When these principles are followed the group remains a safe place for sick people. When they are not followed, the group becomes sick and ineffective. It's the same for churches. When the focus of the church moves away from lost souls coming to know Christ, and becomes a focus of control by the longer term members, then the body becomes sick.

"*Do nothing out of selfish ambition or vain conceit. Rather, in humility value others above yourselves, not looking to your own interests but each of you to the interests of the others. In your relationships with one another, have the same mindset as Christ Jesus.*" Philippians 2:3-5.

In writing the letter to the church at Philippi, Paul describes the mindset of Christ towards people as something we should strive for. It challenges us with an idea, to consider others better than ourselves and to work for their interest as well as ours. It does not say that we forget who we are or look at ourselves as worthless, but it does give a pre-requisite to having the mind of Christ, humility. What an evasive goal being humble is. I heard a man say once that "when you know you're humble, you lost it." Pride will do that to humility.

Applying this verse to ourselves will ensure that we see the newcomer as the most important person in church or recovery. It means that we keep our guard up against "selfish ambition or vain conceit." Our relationships with other people are the measuring tools of how we're doing with this standard. There is a consistency between applying this principle in our lives and the value of personal relationships. People who actively seek to see lost souls come to know Christ seem to have all around good relationships. Recovering addicts who are active in carrying the message of recovery to others seem to have better relationships also. In both cases, this type of person has something to offer. There is something about them that appeal to newcomers. The "old timers" who taught me about recovery used to say, "you see that guy, you don't want what he has." They had nicknames for people with sick recovery, "banner waivers", "parrots", "13th steppers" (in it just to find a relationship), etc. And while these nicknames might seem judgmental, it didn't take long to see people die who learned that type of recovery. These men were trying to save my life, and I was just sick enough to listen and follow directions.

The old timers also said "stick with the winners." I noticed that most of the people with good recovery were involved in service work and always had time for a newcomer. They had what I wanted. Not all people in church and recovery have what I want. For some you can't see the message through the mess. Keep looking around, stick with the winners and most likely they're already involved in service and have a heart for new people.

James 2:26 was a founding scripture of the A.A. program. Bill Wilson lived this scripture just to survive. It is quoted in his story, as the body without the spirit is dead, so "faith without works is dead." His application of this was to work out his faith in God by working with newcomers. And since there weren't any "meetings" yet, he went to where they were. In the hospitals, the streets, shelters, wherever he could find them.

Show me a church or recovery group that emphasizes the importance of the newcomer, and I'll show you a spiritually healthy group of people. Show me the same with a focus on themselves, and I'll show you what anemic faith looks like. Weak and sick, you don't want what they have. Look for the winners, see how they got there, and open your life to their influence. Then pass it on.

#10 - The Power of Testimonies:

The testimony of what God has done in a person's life is one of the most powerful tools we have. Certainly not more powerful than the presence of God in our lives, but when it comes to fulfilling God's calling -- whether to reach the lost, help the addicts, or anything else -- our testimony is a powerful tool. Even advertisers know how powerful a testimony is. Just look at how many commercials try to sell you a product using the "testimony" of someone you don't even know. Even when it's just a script, companies will spend huge amounts of money just to make it look real, because there is power in a testimony.

The Bible is a testimony of God's acts of grace and judgment. It tells of the past, present, and future. Stories from the Old Testament have inspired young people in Sunday School classes for years. They are not just stories. They are testimonies of what God did centuries ago. Noah's Ark, Moses at the Red Sea, David and Goliath, Jonah and the whale, and Sampson and Delilah (maybe for adult Sunday School). Several times in the New Testament the story of God's deliverance of His people from Egypt is retold. There is power in testimonies.

The power of recovery is in the testimonies. The common phrase in support groups is to share "what is was like, what happened, and what it's like now." In meetings people tell the story of what is was like to be hopeless, what happened when God and other addicts entered their life, and what it's like now. In church we are encouraged and challenged by testimonies, especially when someone tells an individually unique story of how God worked in their life. We are motivated to overcome our challenges when we hear how God brought someone else through theirs.

Quite possibly one of the most fascinating aspects of a recovery program is how it actually works. A bunch of people with problems, getting together with other people who have the same problems, working for a common solution. Support groups are really just people giving their testimony. And yet the power of healing and restored relationships abound. Don't underestimate the power of your testimony, God didn't. When He invested His grace and love in your life it was not meant to hide. It was meant to give away by sharing with others. People who feel hopeless need to hear a message of hope. That's what our testimonies do, give hope to others.

Joe E. #1 is a real Christian, just ask him. A former member of a 12 step program, Joe E. #1 saw the light and error of his ways, and off to Bible college he went. Earning a Masters Degree in Theology, he endeavored to set the world straight about its errors on addictions. Unfortunately, Joe E. #1 had relatives in my home church, which meant once a year I could count on seeing him. True to form every year around Christmas time, I would walk into church on a Sunday morning and there he was. He might as well have been decked out in some special ops gear, carrying a weapon with a scope on it, because I was his target. Year after year he tried to correct my testimony and show me the error of my ways.

One year he crossed the line, and told me that if I really understood God's love I wouldn't need recovery. I think he was fortunate that I actually had God's love in my heart. Without it, I would have fell back on my old ways and punched him in the mouth right there in the Sanctuary. Instead, I told him that was strange because recovery helped me to find the depth of God's love, and then I just smiled and walked away. No one can change my testimony or yours. It is an individual matter between each of us and God. He doesn't give me someone else's testimony, nor does He give someone else mine. Hope is transferred when God uses my testimony to invest in the life of another person. My responsibility is to tell the story and give God the glory. Any other method is doomed to fail. Otherwise, I am taking credit for something I didn't deserve in the first place.

Joe E. #1 never changed my testimony, nor was his life ever invested in mine. There was too much arrogance and pride on his part. The truly sad part was that I remember him as a completely arrogant sober alcoholic, obnoxious in meetings, and never quite cleaning up from the inside out. Without resolving those issues, he became a Bible college graduate, an arrogant minister, obnoxious in church and still not clean on the inside. It is too bad he didn't clean up first, because Jesus warned us about this condition.

"Woe to you, teachers of the law and Pharisees, you hypocrites! You are like whitewashed tombs, which look beautiful on the outside but on the inside are full of the bones of the dead and everything unclean." Matthew 23:27.

Joey Starling is a missionary in Nigeria. He and his family left the comforts of life in America to "go" and share the Gospel. He came to my church one Sunday and shared his testimony. After several years of ministering in the same area, he was shot in the face while on his way to church. The injuries were severe and life threatening. He was rushed to the hospital on the back of a moped and lived. After returning stateside to recover, he had a difficult decision to make. Would he go back?

Through conviction of God's will, he and his family returned to Nigeria to the same village. The people who lived there were astonished. They just couldn't believe that he would come back. Joey had shared God's Word with the local people for several years before the attack, but it was the testimony of his return that brought many to Christ in Nigeria. They wanted what he had, and so do I.

The power of Christian faith and genuine recovery is in our testimony.

#11 – Altruism:

This common bond relates closely to the importance of the newcomer, but takes it a step further. By definition, altruism is *"showing an interested and selfless concern for the well-being of others; unselfish."* While this was certainly a core principle of early recovery, it wasn't limited just to working with new people. It was needed for all relationships that the recovering alcoholic had. It relates to how people who have been around for a while and with experience should treat each other.

The Big Book stated that if a person's actions continued to harm others they were quite sure to get drunk. Altruism is what helps people stay sober once they've established sobriety. It's a maintenance type principle helping to keep the conscience clear. The 10th Step in recovery also focuses on keeping life clean, stating that *"when we were wrong, we promptly admitted it."* Ever tried to get a drunk alcoholic or an addict that was high to admit they're wrong? Promptly? If so, then you know firsthand the importance of maintaining an honest evaluation of conduct. It takes a lot of work to clean up a shipwrecked conscience, and it takes regular maintenance to keep it in good condition.

The church can apply all the same principles. Once a person comes to know Christ personally, they have a responsibility to clean up any damage caused by a sinful life. This can be accomplished through the processes of reconciliation and restitution. Once that's done, then regular maintenance becomes the method to stay on track.

Keeping the well-being of others as a standard will ultimately prevent people from becoming complacent, selfish, and ineffective. You don't have to be around a church or recovery program very long to see how losing concern for others can lead to bad decisions. When it becomes all about me, then even Christ comes second. Try attending a business meeting of a church or recovery group, you will find out if that organization has an altruistic focus or not. But the easiest way to gauge the heart of an organization is to observe their treatment of new people. God loves the alcoholic, He loves the addict, and He loves lost souls. He wants us to be the same.

During an interview on Larry King Live, the Reverend Billy Graham was asked a challenging question. The subject of homosexuality came up and the question Larry asked was if Rev. Graham had a son who was homosexual would he still love him as much as his other children. Without hesitation, Rev. Graham said "I would love him more." Genuine altruism will produce that kind of response towards a lost soul or a high addict. It comes from within, and has to be there ahead of time to be effective. Barriers to altruism are removed when the conscience is cleared. It's a character trait that will get you through the storms of life. If you are having a bad day, look outside yourself and give to someone else. Just make sure you have something to give.

At the end of the first 164 pages of the Big Book, the portion known as "The Program," states *"Ask Him in your morning meditation what you can do each day for the man who is still sick. The answers will come, if your own house is in order. But obviously you cannot transmit something you haven't got. See to it that your relationship with Him is right, and great events will come to pass for you and countless others."* Altruism is a core standard for both the church and recovery programs. Without it, the process is compromised and the finished product will not look anything like the original intent. If this is the case, return to the core standards which established the original quality. Adjust to the current world without compromising the standards. Great events will come to pass for you and countless others.

#12 - Singular Purpose:

There is truly a singular purpose to the church and recovery. The common bond here is not that they have the same purpose, but that ultimately the purpose is singular.

For churches, it is the Gospel, the death, burial, and resurrection of Jesus Christ. It is about ministering to people who are born on this earth, but have yet to be born again, the spiritual birth Jesus described to Nicodemus in John Chapter 3. It is all about eternity, putting aside the weight of this world with its struggles to show someone the path to eternal life. Christianity "goes" into all the world to share this message of hope. And when selfish people ask the common question, "why go around the world when we have problems here," we can say with calm assurance that we do both. The "Great Commission" in Matthew 28:20 gives three places to go, Jerusalem, Judea, and all the world. In other words, locally, regionally, and internationally. People who understand this do not ask the question, they already know the answer from living out the purpose of the church.

For recovery it's about sobriety, the life changing message of deliverance through a process. Substitute the problem for any another and it's the same goal, eliminate it from your life permanently. It's about establishing a relationship with God, cleaning up the damage, and letting Him use you to help others. It is not the path to eternal life, but it will make your life here free from the destruction of addiction. And the reason we go anywhere God opens the door to share the message of hope, is because people all over the world are struggling with the same problems. We help people locally, regionally, and internationally, because that is where God is. He does both, and so do we.

The quickest way to lose focus overall is to lose focus on the singular purpose. Tradition #5 of recovery programs states that "*each group has but one primary purpose; to carry its message to the alcoholic who still suffers.*" This standard, this principle of recovery, has served groups and programs well in keeping focus on what's important. It seems that a version of this would be good for church by-laws, *"each church has but one primary purpose; to take the Gospel to the soul who is still without Christ."*

In closing for this chapter, it is worth noting one other principle: no graduation before death. At funerals, sometimes the transition from this life to the next is called "graduation," and most certainly it is. But until that day there's no retirement, and no graduation from the body of Christ. As long as we have breath, we have responsibility to share the Gospel. The same principle exists in recovery. There's no diploma, no ceremony, no graduation. You're in it for life, it will end at your last breath. Some people see recovery as a life sentence, but it's really a life privilege.

CHAPTER SEVEN

··

Never Say Never, Just Say "Yet"

The seventh and final principle is simple but with a broad application. Everyone is not an addict, but everyone has the potential to become one. Denying this is futile; there are too many testimonies to prove otherwise. Even if a person does manage to avoid the pitfalls of addiction, what about their family? It's hard to find someone, anyone, who is not affected by addiction. Divorce, crime, prison, and death are just a few of the outcomes that bring pain and suffering into the lives of addicts and their families. Is it really worth saying "it will never happen to me," when the risk is so high? Never say never, just say yet.

From the time the first act of violence was committed, God has been telling us to beware. Before Cain killed Abel, God spoke the words that we need to remember today:

"If you do what is right, will you not be accepted? But if you do not do what is right, sin is crouching at your door; it desires to have you, but you must master it." Genesis 4:6.

"This dread warning to Cain, expressed in the mildest and plainest terms, is a standing lesson written for the learning of all mankind." Commentary by Barnes.

Sin is crouching at the door. It is trying to stay out of sight but is close by; always ready to ambush anyone at anytime. Cain ignored God's advice, and paid a permanent price for his rejection of the truth. So will we if we try to claim that Christians are above such things as addiction, because sin is waiting for anyone to forget that its crouching at *their* door. There are no exceptions. Only those in denial who say "we don't have those kinds of problems."

There's an abundance of testimonies from people who lived most of their lives without any struggles with addiction, only to find themselves or a family member hooked on drugs or alcohol. Some start when they have a surgery or medical procedure, begin using prescription pain pills for post surgery recovery, and find later they can't let go of the pills once the intended use is complete. Other examples are from people who are already in a recovery program, who later take prescribed medicine and then relapse. They let their guard down and trigger the thorn in the flesh. And even if the family is free from addiction of any kind, someone could be the first. There are people who have established recovery for their primary addiction, only to find out later they need additional recovery for codependency or a secondary addiction. The possibilities seem endless.

The only consistent thing about addiction is its inconsistency.

Jane E. #8 is a woman who drank herself into a recovery program. Working hard at her recovery, she was able to succeed in staying clean and sober for nearly two years. One night she went out to dinner at a first class restaurant. When the salad was served she smelled something in the dressing and knew it was alcohol, but went ahead and ate it anyway. The physical element of addiction was triggered and Jane E. #8 ordered a drink. After relapsing and returning to her recovery program, she admitted that she had taken her sobriety for granted. What she forgot was that sin was crouching at the door and desired to have her. She started saying never, and should have been saying yet.

Our local newspaper will occasionally run an article called "Take 5." The paper will produce five questions for a selected individual to answer, and then publish the questions along with the responses. The topics are a way for the community to learn more about local organizations. I was asked by the paper to "Take 5" on our local recovery ministry. One of the questions fits well into the seventh principle Christians need to know:

Q: How can you measure the toll of drug and alcohol abuse and other addictions in terms of the human cost?

A: Some have paid the ultimate price. One is enough. It is said that for every one addict, 14 other people are affected. Whether the literal number is true doesn't matter, the principle is. Alcohol and drug abuse takes a toll on people that can't be measured, but the results are evident – broken families, children without parents, violence, abuse and crime. Maybe 14 is a low number.

John E. #10 is a man who never drank until he was in his mid 40's. He is a committed Christian and a very successful businessman. Within 4 years of his first drink he was in detox, then treatment, and started a trend of continually relapsing with alcohol. Despite the threat of loss of family, vocation and his own life, he just continued an addictive cycle. Several times John E. #10 went to treatment, always with renewed hope for staying sober but would eventually get drunk. His outcome has "yet" to be determined; but the options are disappearing, and life and death are now hanging in the balance.

Never say never, just say yet.

In the late 1990's, a state trooper from Tennessee was speaking at our church one Sunday. There was a time before the main service where he shared some testimonies and allowed for questions. After spending several years in law enforcement he was assigned to Vice, specifically in the sexual abuse division. The testimony of his first three arrests was shocking: a preacher, a deacon, and a man who had a large sign in his front yard that said "Jesus Saves." He said two years was about the most any officer could work in that division, the impact was so harsh.

I doubt those three men ever thought they would be arrested, but they were. Sin had not only been crouching at their door, but they had let it in. No more "yet's," just consequences for hurting others. They can never go back and change what happened. At some point a person in these circumstances must think back to a time before sin conceived and gave birth to death, and wish they had made better choices.

"People do not despise a thief if he steals to satisfy his hunger when he is starving. Yet if he is caught, he must pay sevenfold, though it costs him all the wealth of his house. But a man who commits adultery has no sense; whoever does so, destroys himself. Blows and disgrace are his lot, and his shame will never be wiped away." Proverbs 6:30-33.

"For everything in the world—the lust of the flesh, the lust of the eyes, and the pride of life—comes not from the Father but from the world." I John 2:16.

"You have heard that it was said, 'You shall not commit adultery.' But I tell you that anyone who looks at a woman lustfully has already committed adultery with her in his heart." Matthew 5:27-28.

Philip Yancey is an American Christian author. To date, 14 million copies of his books have been sold worldwide, and he is recognized as a best-selling evangelical author. Philip was the keynote speaker for the annual Overcomers Outreach convention that was held in LaGrange, IL. During his session, he stated that about 60% of Christian men in evangelical churches were hooked on pornography. I was on the Board of Directors for Overcomers at the time and was aware that 80% of the calls coming into our central office were from men struggling with sexual issues. Mark Laasar, a leading Christian author on the subject of sexual addiction, was also on the Board of Overcomers and in attendance at the conference in La Grange. He agreed with Philip Yancey's estimate. That was around the year 2000, and the problem hasn't decreased, yet.

It takes tremendous courage for a person struggling with an addictive problem to ask for help. For quite some time it's been a major risk to do so in the church because you might get help to follow Jesus in the crucifixion. Not literally but close enough, especially if you're in a leadership role. Call it denial or whatever you want; the Christian church has been the equivalent of an ostrich when it comes to sexual addiction.

The volatility of calling it an addiction has raised the same old objections that used to be used for alcohol and drugs. "What used to be called immorality is now called a disease." Or simply, "what is the world coming to?" While the world around us just continually modifies its standards to justify sin, the church actually has the answer but far too many won't use it. Such contempt for a subject the Bible speaks volumes about.

An article published on Christian Drug Rehab's website about sexual addiction in the church stated *"Being a Christian and knowing the power of Christ means that we have hope in overcoming sin and temptation, not that you will be magically free of it. Satan is at work in the world and there is nothing he loves more than to drag a believer down. Sex is an easy avenue."*

This article is actually titled "Women, Sex Addiction and the Church" with a subtitle of "Female Sex Addicts? In the Church?" When A.A. started it was mostly men, but didn't stay that way very long. Such is the case with sexual addictions.

Recovery programs have taken the lead with this issue. Several have come into existence using the same recovery model as A.A. as a solution, and it works. Just like with the beginnings of A.A., most of the people seeking these programs are either Christians already or they are seeking God through these programs. Churches are starting to recognize the problem and are taking steps to be a true New Testament Church, showing through their actions what they believe in their hearts. If the church is a hospital for sinners, then the emergency entrance has to be open when the wounded arrive. Contempt closes the door and it might as well just be out of business. A Christian can be a sex addict, and besides the obvious physical expression, the main chemical behind sexual addiction is actually produced by the brain. There is a physical element of sexual addiction.

At one point around 1999, our recovery ministry had several support group meetings at the same time each week. It was a very active ministry that had groups for alcoholics, drug addicts, codependents, food addictions, a teen group, and a sexual addiction group, with the full support of our church leaders and pastor. The contempt by some of our church members revealed a few misconceptions about addictions. First, some people thought because I led the ministry that I attended all the groups. Wow, "a teenage alcoholic codependent addicted to sex, drugs, and food." How in the world anyone could think such a thing was actually quite humorous, but it really showed how little some Christians know about addiction. Sometimes you just have to laugh, because there's no other sane response to the insanity.

Secondly, the contempt went right to the pastor's office. Quite a few people objected to having a support group for sexual addictions at our church. "Steve is bringing child molesters and pedophiles into the church and endangering our children," was the complaint. One of our deacons, a true and genuine Christian man, spoke with one of the people giving this objection and offered wisdom. "You don't have to worry about the people going to those groups. What you need to worry about are the ones sitting next to you on Sunday morning doing nothing about their problem."

The pastor didn't say who made the comments, but in a conversation in his office with this deacon and myself he mentioned what was being said. My response, "Bringing sinners to church, what a concept." The idea of protecting the church by not having a recovery program for sexual addictions is a false standard, because what it really accomplishes is making the church a "hide out" for child molesters and pedophiles, which really endangers the children. The church for quite some time has been the easiest way for perverts to gain access to children. No questions asked if you want to help take care of the kids, just come on in. Churches practicing truth have taken the proper steps, screening people who volunteer to work with children and creating systems of accountability. It's a revealing truth that churches who are taking steps to protect children are often the same ones with recovery programs. No false standards, just the truth, the whole truth, and nothing but the truth. Let's face it. Would a pervert who is hiding in darkness try to go into a church that is shining the light on sexual sins? It is possible, but it is much safer to put on a mask and go into a church that's in denial.

The Christian church is repeating history in the sense of responding to sexual addictions the same way it responded to drug and alcohol addictions. Some churches are trying to help those who are seeking freedom through recovery and the Bible, but many are using the same old phrases. The sleeping giant just keeps hitting the snooze button while the problem gets worse. And since the church overall didn't respond at the right time, God gave the responsibility to the sex addicts, the despised and the rejected ones.

The timing also shows a repeat of history. The 1960's in America were not only characterized by drug abuse, but also a "sexual revolution" which promised freedom to express your sexuality in whatever made you feel good. And much like the roaring 20's, followed by the introduction of the first recovery program for alcoholism, the 1960's were followed by the first recovery program for sexual addiction. The false standard of freedom had led to captivity. The first program, Sexaholics Anonymous, started developing in the 1970's and was officially recognized in 1979. Patrick Carnes groundbreaking book about sexual addiction, "Out of the Shadows", was written in 1983. Several other recovery programs for sexual addictions have since been introduced using the same recovery model that originated with A.A. All of this information is readily available on the internet; only contempt would keep someone from investigating.

Yet the problem got worse. 1988 was the introduction of the first pill to overcome male impotence, and we have been inundated with "ask your doctor" ever since. The human body has become a science experiment for chemicals to grow hair, rev up your sex life, increase memory and testosterone, burn fat, etc. Not much different from the claims traveling salesmen made in the mid 1800's about how their miracle cures would remedy all manner of illnesses. We look back at these people with sarcastic humor, but maybe that is how the coming generations will look at ours for believing in so many miracle cures. And the only real difference is technology, which some people worship as the source of all truth. For some, they have created their own god, the "goat" (god of advanced technology), and do they ever worship their god. But only the one true God is all knowing (omniscient) and all powerful (omnipotent). Proper medications are a blessing, but a pill to solve every problem is just another smoke screen from the father of lies to hide his progress with lust and sexual sin.

Prohibition won't work. Having an earthly king won't work. Having individual responsibility for actions will. Today, we have people trying to create rules that women cannot wear certain clothes in public. Meanwhile, thousands of young girls are abducted into sex slavery every year. Some cry for the government to do something, while at the same time they reject God's standards and claim the right to do whatever they want. Only those who take individual responsibility for their problems are finding a solution, and God is at the center. In general, Christians are getting distracted in the storm of lust, and cannot see the solution from the problem. The majority think sexual addiction recovery is part of the problem, which is just another example of attributing the works of God to the character of Satan.

This subject is also being studied at nausea, resulting in many attempts to justify sin, or treat our God given sexual desires as an experiment. God's standards are being ignored. Meanwhile, most churches don't even want to say the word sex from the pulpit. Maybe they don't have those kinds of problems, or maybe they have become a safe place for child molesters and pedophiles to hide. Some have been arguing for so long they have become master debaters, engaged in self-gratification for the benefit of no one else, but it does make them feel good.

People who deal with lust by trying to control it are foolish. Satan knows its power, which is why he used it in the Garden of Eden to tempt Adam and Eve. It was the desire for what was being offered that convinced Eve to let the seed of sin enter her life, as well as Adam. They should have held to the standard God gave them, to not experience something that would hurt them. Trying to make up a bunch of rules to control these desires does not work. Most of the time these rules are intended to control other people so that someone doesn't "cause" another to sin. Blame is not the answer to lust. Adam and Eve already tried that. The world we live in seems to run between two extremes when it comes to lust, to over indulge or suppress the desire. Neither one will work.

Christians need to understand what every advertising agency already knows, sex sells. Lust is the most effective tool available to sell a product, providing fantasies, lies, and an image of what could be. All you need is a product in your life, something to enter from the outside. These thoughts are a function of the carnal mind, and advertisers spend millions of dollars to get into your head, at least one part of it. The goal is to burn a desire or image into your memory that will affect your decisions. But how much of advertising is based on reality? It's really about fantasy, and it works. Take a close look at advertisements whether in print or video, and sort out the fantasy from the real. The challenge will be to find anything that is based on reality. At best, it will be some lustful fantasy about what people would like for their reality to be.

The majority of sexual content in advertising is the use of women's bodies to sell merchandise. A woman's value is based on her curves, proportions, and facial attraction. But not for all women. It is just those who are good enough to generate fantasy and lust in the minds of others. A woman's breasts and back sides are the best tool for sparking the lust fire which can lead to selling a product. And if you are a woman whose proportions don't merit such value, then our culture has plenty of derogatory statements about you relating to animals. So how does that make you feel ladies? Not good enough to be lust worthy, or full of pride that you can measure up to a false standard. God's standards are replaced by false standards, because He looks at the heart and not the flesh. The world's standard for beauty constantly changes. God has his own standard that never changes, and He loves you unconditionally apart from physical appearance. Jesus died for your heart and soul, not your flesh. The power of lust through advertising is replacing God's value in women, and the church sleeps on the subject of sex as an addiction.

"Charm is deceptive, and beauty is fleeting, but a woman who fears the Lord is to be praised." Proverbs 31:30.

Sexual addiction recovery programs are vastly different from the sexual standards of rest of the world. No substitute chemicals to solve the problem, no creation of your own god, just Biblical truth through the 12 Steps providing deliverance through a process. No room for Naamanites; only the weak looking for God's grace. The common standards between recovery programs and the church have been upheld with sexual addiction recovery.

Yet after the first recovery program for sex was established, it didn't take long for people to get off track, just as in the first recovery program and the first century church. Today, there are several programs using the 12 Steps for sexual addictions, each with a slightly different definition of "sobriety." In general, these are referred to as "S" programs. Again, anyone can easily research this information on the internet. The only "S" program that has a sobriety definition that is consistent with Biblical standards is Sexaholics Anonymous, the original "S" program. Most of the other programs were created due to rejection of the S.A. standard, which is to have no sex outside of marriage. Within 10 years of this program's beginning came the challenges to the definition, mostly from people who want to redefine marriage. According to a Wikipedia website page:

"SA helps recovering "sexaholics." According to the group, a sexaholic is someone for whom "lust has become an addiction."[1] Thus SA distinguishes itself from other S groups by defining sexual sobriety as no sex with self or with partners other than with one's spouse and a progressive victory over lust. SA received permission from AA to use its Twelve Steps and Twelve Traditions in 1979,[4] (Wikipedia).

The problem of sexual addiction centers in the mind. In fact, the chemicals produced by the brain are the intoxicating elements that produce the "high." These internal chemicals were created by God for a purpose, for the pleasure of physical intimacy. When these chemicals are released at the proper time under the standards that God established, then it is a blessing to experience. However, when through our own desires we are "dragged away and enticed," and these chemicals are released at the wrong time for an ungodly purpose, there is only sin that leads to death. If a person continues violating God's standards they will cross a line into addiction, but instead of having to buy external substances they can produce their own chemicals through lust. And as stated in James Chapter 1, *"Then, after desire has conceived, it gives birth to sin, and sin, when it is full grown, gives birth to death."*

Perhaps the solution is to bring back the old fashioned standards. I doubt any thoughtful Christian would really want that, given the polluted history of old fashioned standards. It's easy to think that everything old fashioned is better than what we have today, but consider that the following was once perceived as truth:

"By the Middles Ages it was a sin to have sex with a child. If an adult were guilty of such a sin, one remedy was to declare the child a witch. The child thus became an offender who 'beguiled' the adult with the power of the Evil One. Understanding this process puts a new light on the burning of witches. A Catholic bishop in Wurttemberg in the seventeenth century writes, for example, of his sadness at having presided over the burning of three hundred young girls that year and wondered if the churches were making a mistake.

"By the nineteenth century, society had given up burning witches. Yet the sexual exploitation of children continued. In late nineteenth century in Britain, for example, men who raped young girls were excused because they did it to cure venereal disease. There was a widely held belief that children would take 'poisons' out of the body. In fact, leprosy, venereal disease, depression, and impotence were part of a wide range of maladies believed cured by having sex with the young. An English medical text of the time reads "Breaking a maiden's seal is one of the best antidotes for one's ills. Cudgeling her unceasingly, until she swoons away, is a mighty remedy for man's depression. It cures all impotence." Quotes from: Sexual Anorexia: Overcoming Sexual Self-Hatred. Patrick J. Carnes.

How's your gut feel? It's sickening to think that society and even churches have not only condoned such contempt and ignorance, but actually initiated it. Some might see a way out by claiming this is in the past, that "we don't have those kinds of problems." Author Steven R. Tracy has written several books on the subject of abuse from a Christian perspective, including sexual abuse. In his book "Mending the Soul" which was first published in 2005, he writes about an American Christian missionary who died in a foreign country while serving Christ. The public version is that he was killed as a martyr for his faith. The truth is he was a child molester who had hurt a lot of children over many years.

He was actually murdered in a foreign jail after being arrested for sexually abusing a child. Stated on their website is the description of the book's contents:

"Abuse can be sexual, physical, neglect, spiritual, and verbal. The chief arguments pursued throughout the book are: (1) abuse is far more rampant than most Christians realize, but due to human depravity and satanic influence, widespread abuse is predictable. (2) All types of abuse create profound, long-term soul damage due to the way abuse perverts various aspects of the image of God. (3) God is the healing redeemer. Human salvation came through horrible physical abuse. (4) Healing must take place in the context of relationships. Humans are deeply impacted by others due to being made in the image of God. Just as surely as abusive relationships have tremendous power to wound the soul, so healthy relationships have tremendous power to nurture and heal the soul." Mending the Soul by Stephen R. Tracy.

Today, the sexual exploitation of woman and children is epidemic. Trafficking has made human beings the new drug. Organizations that formerly moved bundles of marijuana and cocaine now move people, but those bundles never had a soul. Other people have found the lust and wealth of exploiting people irresistible, they are wolves in sheep's clothing who live without conscience. The church is beginning to respond.

The sleeping giant is waking up. Yet the problem has increased.

As Christians, we have the answer because *"there is nothing new under the sun"* (Ecclesiastes 3:11,) but if we refuse to use it God will give it to someone else. It's time to wake up and fight the good fight of faith, letting go of the right to be right, especially when souls are at stake. But first we have to identify why the subject of unity in the body of Christ is actually preventing the solution from being used.

There's a story in Russia relating to the Christian church that reflects truth. It seems there was a problem in one of the large cities in Russia with squirrels. The city had become overrun with these pesky varmints and the city officials went to the churches to ask for help. First, the city went to the Baptist church, but they were too busy praying and reading their Bibles to help. Next, the city went to the Charismatic church, and they laid hands on the squirrels and cast them out. But soon the squirrels were back, so the city went to the Catholic church and the problem was solved. They baptized all the squirrels and now you only see them on Christmas and Easter.

Substitute addict for squirrel and it fits just fine. Churches function within communities with the ability to address problems that are plaguing society. The Baptist's have gained a reputation of addressing addiction primarily through prayer and Bible reading only, to an extreme. While these two elements are necessary to achieve recovery, limiting the effort to just these two will only work with students attending School of Addiction 1, therefore non-addicts. The Charismatics have gained a reputation of seeking a one step method of quick and spectacular deliverance, just like Naaman expected in I Kings. Again, this will work for non-addicts from School 1. Both of these are methods of being delivered in moment, which will work for many who struggle with life's problems, but it won't work for addicts who have acquired the physical disease of addiction. The Catholics have held to the truth about alcoholism and addiction for quite some time. The late Father Joseph Martin was a prolific speaker about alcoholism. His materials are still being used to help addicts learn the truth about addiction; his "Chalk Talks" are freely available through the internet. The main issue with the Catholic church is there seems to be a lot people who claim the faith but are "not practicing." They're isolated, but do seem to show up at least twice a year.

A Russian church in a large city had asked for help in starting a recovery ministry. In a city of 500,000 people, it was estimated that 50% or greater were alcoholics or addicts. The influence was visible everywhere. I traveled there initially with some other Christians to provide teaching and support, and for the next several years I went there every six months to continue the work. God was blessing in mighty ways and the recovery ministry in this church was growing exponentially in numbers and influence. Drunks were getting sober, addicts were getting clean, and families were learning to stop enabling. God was truly being glorified. Part of the support was to conduct a seminar during each trip to continue the teaching and training. The only problem was this church didn't have a building, so they rented various buildings which included churches from other denominations.

With success comes recognition, and a U.S. based Russian television station ran a story about the events in this city. Some of the Christians living in the U.S. saw that the church from their denomination was renting its building to this church from a different denomination. The response was to threaten withdrawal of financial support if they didn't cut off the other church from using their building. So the response from the right arm of the body of Christ was to cut off the left arm and see if it could survive on its own. Unbelievable. When God's people refuse to do His work, He will find someone else. The Lord provided another building and the work continued. It seems that the squirrel church was full of nuts, ones that wanted to be part of the problem and not the solution. Just interested in finding other nuts like themselves, in the name of Jesus.

Never say that we have done enough in the church for the problems of addiction. Just say we haven't done enough yet. Sin has many faces. It will move from substance to substance, from one issue to another. Where progress has been made with recovery for drugs and alcohol, ground has been lost to the "lust of the flesh" through sexual problems. Over the last few decades, a large part of the church has awakened to the drug and alcohol problems only to hide from the sexual addiction issues. Meanwhile, clergy lose their ministries, some are arrested, the church gets a damaged testimony, and innocent victims are scarred spiritually. Instead of coasting we should press on with the progress that's been made, and increase our influence with the message of hope. Those who have not opened their doors to recovery should do one thing, forget what is behind. It's time to wake up. We do not have to live in our past failures. *"Brothers and sisters, I do not consider myself yet to have taken hold of it. But one thing I do: Forgetting what is behind and straining toward what is ahead."* Philippians 3:13.

It starts with replacing false standards with truth. Then the person who is sitting in church on Sunday's, hiding their problem, can seek help. This is not a theory, it's happened already in churches that have put aside false standards and strive to be like Christ, to love the way He loves, because *"while we were still sinners, Christ died for us."* (Romans 5:8).

One thing we can count on is addiction will change its face. Every time a new drug becomes the latest choice or the cheapest high, we don't have to come up with a new solution. Recovery is from the Bible. It will work on any issue that becomes the next addiction. Whether it's the drugs of past, the newest pill, a cheaper heroin, or yet another way to get drunk, recovery remains the same. Even if the problem is gambling, sex, pornography or even codependency, recovery still works. It always will.

We do not know what the next addiction is going to be. It might come after we have departed from this world. But we can absolutely agree that Satan will produce yet another addictive issue at some point in the future. The evil one never says never, he just says yet, because he knows that his time is limited but hasn't run out, yet. Will Christianity be ready for the next addiction? Will we go back to sleep? Are we going to be a blessing or a curse to our children's children? Will you be the one who decides to become the second generation? My former pastor used to say "The decisions that we make are the hinges of the doors upon which our future swings." Our decisions will either open the door or close it.

The greatest impact of human change starts with one person. History has repeated itself over and over on this point.

A Christian's prime example is Jesus Christ, who came into the world to cause change, and the world has never been the same since. He worked with others, they in turn carried the message to the masses. Many others have followed suit. Martin Luther was inspired by God's standard that the "just shall live by faith." Bill Wilson was compelled to believe that "faith without works was dead." Each was a person with a desire to cause change, who worked with others that in turn carried the message to countless others. There is only one Christ, but there are many examples of those who used His methods. We each have the same opportunity, regardless of our genetics or the influences in our lives. We have choices, and the ones we make will determine the risk of living our lives as debaters, modern day Pharisees, or self-governing agents of change. No committee or study needed; just individual faith combined with works.

When pride is put in front of human beings then we elevate the creation. When error is recognized and change is made to honor God, then we bring glory to our Creator, and that is worship. Otherwise, we have *"exchanged the truth for a lie, and worship and serve created things rather than the Creator – who is forever praised. Amen."* Romans 1:25.

Are you going to worship the creation or the Creator?
Stop saying never, just say yet.
I don't have an addiction, yet.
No one in my family is an addict, yet.
My life hasn't been affected by addictions, yet.
I don't understand addictions, yet.
I have never relapsed, yet.
We don't have those problems at our church, yet.
Our church will be open for the addict we have never met, yet.
Some of this breaks through the denial,
others are simply acceptance of the possibility.
All are truth.

As the church, the Body of Christ:

- We cannot repeat our mistakes that were made with other addictions.
- We must do better, and take the lead in helping people with all addictions.
- Lead the change on addictions, starting with sex addiction, and planting the seeds for the future.
- We must remain open to all types of problems, not just certain ones.
- We must embrace a solution that God Himself has embraced, recovery.
- Speak words of life, and prove our love for the suffering by our actions.
- We have to remember that God has a plan for each person's life; we are not the interpreters, just the servants.
- Treat secular recovery as a chance to share the Gospel, and quit saying nebulous.
- Above all, do what God tells you to do individually. You might have to be the first.

Outreach:

- Change the attitude from acceptance of addicts to pursuing. One is an expression of spirituality, the other is an act of love. It needs to be more than just allowing the use of a building, they need to be welcomed and shown the love of Christ.
- Ask two people to give a testimony to the church at the same time, one from School of Addiction 1 and another from School of Addiction 3. Only contempt would prevent this from happening.

- Offer your facility for a recovery meeting, event, conference, or special speaker. Recovery programs pay their own way according to the 7th Tradition, how much they pay often depends on the other organization. Some try to make money off the addicts, others keep it at a minimum of one dollar per year, meeting, or event.
- Have an annual Recovery Sunday Service dedicated to this work in your community.
- Add a School 1 or 3 treatment program to your mission's support.

Referrals:

We are only as good as our referrals. No one can be all things to all people, but we can surround ourselves with referrals. The best method of finding recovery or treatment programs is to call one. This method works for people who are looking for help, families who are trying to find a program for a loved one, or someone just building their referral base. Every program knows of at least one other program. So start with one call, get information about that program, and ask for a referral to another program. Keep repeating the sequence. It won't take long before you have an extensive list that will meet a multitude of needs.

All clergy should have a list of referrals, as well anyone interested in being part of the solution. It is not just the leaders' responsibility to know where to find help. Waiting until a person shows up with an addiction to find out where the resources are is wasted time. The chemicals in an addict's mind will shift before you can find the resource. Be ready in season and out of season. Each Christian should have at least one contact who understands addiction, so they can give a referral anytime it's needed. Keep in mind that it is not our responsibility to pre-determine which method God will use for the individual. We are servants who need to discern God's will, not our own. Referral lists should include as many good resources as you can find.

- ➤ The Church needs leaders who recognize an addict when they see one and make a referral, to either a 12 step program or treatment center. Discerning whether it's a School 1 or School 3 referral should be the goal.
- ➤ School 1 needs to make referrals to School 3, and School 3 to School 1.
- ➤ Make referrals when it's beyond your abilities, not God's, just yours.
- ➤ Find out where the good resources are so you don't make a bad referral. Not all programs, counselors, and treatment centers are good. Investigate, ask others, and build a solid referral list.

What every Christian needs to know about Addictions:

Biblical truth for replacement of false standards reiterated:

- Some People are Delivered in a Moment, Others are Delivered Through a Process
- A Christian Can be an Addict
- There is a Physical Element of Addiction
- Addicts Must Remember Their Past
- 12 Step Recovery is not a path to Heaven, or Hell
- There are 12 Common Bonds between Recovery and Church
- Never Say Never, Just Say "Yet".

We are all delivered from something,
but we are not delivered from all things.
If you seek the Father, you will find the Son.
A solution is only as good as it holds up under the worst
of circumstances.
For the person dying of addiction in the pews, there is hope.
Some people see recovery as a life sentence,
but it's really a life privilege.
Jesus Christ is a simple solution to a complicated problem,
acceptance of the solution is our problem.
When it comes to addiction, for every rule there's an exception.
The only consistent thing about addiction is its inconsistency.
The negative voice is always loud.
The power of recovery is in our testimonies.
The closer we get to the mark, the farther away it is.
Just being the opposite of what is wrong doesn't make you right.
The second generation is the opportunity for change.
God chose the undesirable to reach the unreachable,
and the result was uncontainable.

Anytime we have a chance to help someone with an
addiction, or a family member learn about their faith or lack of,
and ask God for discernment to know the answer to this question:
Can such a faith save him? (*or her*) James 2:14.

If they're struggling with life, call School 1,
If they're an addict, call School 3.
If you don't know, use referrals.
Never say never.
Just say yet.
Their life may depend on it.

....

Overcomers Outreach

http://www.overcomersoutreach.org/, National Office,
12828 Acheson Dr., Whittier, CA 90601,
Toll Free 1-800-310-3001, Local (562) 698-9000

Celebrate Recovery

http://www.celebraterecovery.com/

Teen Challenge

http://teenchallengeusa.com/ **TEEN CHALLENGE USA,**
5250 N Towne Center Dr., Ozark, Missouri 65721,
(417) 581-2181, 855-END-ADDICTION,
info@teenchallengeusa.com

New Life

http://newlife.com/

NEW LIFE MINISTRIES

PO Box 1018, Laguna Beach CA 92652, 949-494-8383,
800-NEW-LIFE (639-5433)

Alcoholics Anonymous

http://www.aa.org/, AA General Service Office,
307 7th Ave #201, New York, NY, (212) 647-1680

Narcotics Anonymous

http://www.na.org/, NA World Services, PO Box 9999, Van Nuys, California USA 91409, Telephone +1.818.773.9999, Fax +1.818.700.0700

Sexaholics Anonymous

http://www.sa.org/, Sexaholics Anonymous International Central Office, PO Box 3565, Brentwood, TN 37024, Phone (615) 370-6062, Toll-free (866) 424-8777, Fax (615) 370-0882, Email saico@sa.org

Al-Anon Family Groups

http://www.al-anon.org/, Al-Anon Family Group Headquarters, Inc., 1600 Corporate Landing Parkway, Virginia Beach, VA 23454-5617, Telephone (757) 563-1600, Fax (757) 563-1656, email: wso@al-anon.org

Other National Hotlines: Search the internet for your local area using the program name. Look in the White Pages of your local directory.